Mathematics Higher Level
Topic 8 – Option:
Sets, Relations and Groups
for the IB Diploma

Paul Fannon, Vesna Kadelburg, Ben Woolley and Stephen Ward

CAMBRIDGE
UNIVERSITY PRESS

CAMBRIDGE
UNIVERSITY PRESS

University Printing House, Cambridge CB2 8BS, United Kingdom

Cambridge University Press is part of the University of Cambridge.

It furthers the University's mission by disseminating knowledge in the pursuit of education, learning and research at the highest international levels of excellence.

www.cambridge.org
Information on this title: www.cambridge.org/9781107646285

© Cambridge University Press 2013

First published 2013
Reprinted 2014

Printed in Poland by Opolgraf

A catalogue record for this publication is available from the British Library

ISBN 978-1-107-64628-5 Paperback

Cover image: Thinkstock

Cambridge University Press has no responsibility for the persistence or accuracy of URLs for external or third-party internet websites referred to in this publication, and does not guarantee that any content on such websites is, or will remain, accurate or appropriate. Information regarding prices, travel timetables and other factual information given in this work is correct at the time of first printing but Cambridge University Press does not guarantee the accuracy of such information thereafter.

....

Contents

How to use this book   iv

Introduction   1

1   Preliminaries: Proof by contradiction   3

2   Sets and operations   6
2A   Defining sets   6
2B   Operations   12
2C   Operations on sets   25

3   Ordered pairs, relations and functions   37
3A   Ordered pairs   37
3B   Binary relations and numerical congruence   40
3C   Classifying relations   43
3D   Functions   50

4   Groups and subgroups   67
4A   Group structure   67
4B   Group properties and cyclic groups   71
4C   Subgroups and cosets   79
4D   Lagrange's theorem   86
4E   Frequently encountered groups   89
4F   Homomorphisms and kernels   101
4G   Isomorphisms   109

5   Summary and mixed examination practice   119

Supplementary sheet: Groups of order 6   125

Answers   127

Glossary   134

Index   141

Acknowledgements   144

How to use this book

Structure of the book

This book covers all the material for Topic 8 (Sets, Relations and Groups Option) of the Higher Level Mathematics syllabus for the International Baccalaureate course. It is largely independent of the Core material, although some examples use vectors and complex numbers; the only real pre-requisite is familiarity with functions (syllabus topic 2.1), though you will also find it beneficial to cover proof by induction (syllabus topic 1.4) and sets and Venn diagrams (syllabus topics 5.2 and 5.3). We have tried to include in the main text only the material that will be examinable. There are many interesting applications and ideas that go beyond the syllabus and we have tried to highlight some of these in the 'From another perspective' and 'Research explorer' boxes.

The material is roughly split into three blocks (sets and operations; functions and relations; groups), and those are contained in chapters 2 to 4. Chapter 1 introduces some methods of mathematical proof that are used throughout the course. Chapter 5 contains a summary of all the topics and further examination practice, with many of the questions mixing several topics – a favourite trick in IB examinations.

Each chapter starts with a list of learning objectives to give you an idea about what the chapter contains. There is an introductory problem at the start of the topic that illustrates what you should be able to do after you have completed the topic. At the start, you should not expect to be able to solve the problem, but you may want to think about possible strategies and what sort of new facts and methods would help you. The solution to the introductory problem is provided at the end of chapter 5.

Key point boxes

The most important ideas and formulae are emphasised in the 'KEY POINT' boxes. When the formulae are given in the Formula booklet, there will be an icon: ▮; if this icon is not present, then the formulae are **not** in the Formula booklet and you may need to learn them or at least know how to derive them.

Worked examples

Each worked example is split into two columns. On the right is what you should write down. Sometimes the example might include more detail then you strictly need, but it is designed to give you an idea of what is required to score full method marks in examinations. However, mathematics is about much more than examinations and remembering methods. So, on the left of the worked examples are notes that describe the thought processes and suggest which route you should use to tackle the question. We hope that these will help you with any exercise questions that differ from the worked examples. It is very deliberate that some of the questions require you to do more than repeat the methods in the worked examples. Mathematics is about thinking!

Signposts

There are several boxes that appear throughout the book.

Theory of knowledge issues

Every lesson is a Theory of knowledge lesson, but sometimes the links may not be obvious. Mathematics is frequently used as an example of certainty and truth, but this is often not the case. In these boxes we will try to highlight some of the weaknesses and ambiguities in mathematics as well as showing how mathematics links to other areas of knowledge.

From another perspective

The International Baccalaureate® encourages looking at things in different ways. As well as highlighting some international differences between mathematicians these boxes also look at other perspectives on the mathematics we are covering: historical, pragmatic and cultural.

Research explorer

As part of your course, you will be asked to write a report on a mathematical topic of your choice. It is sometimes difficult to know which topics are suitable as a basis for such reports, and so we have tried to show where a topic can act as a jumping-off point for further work. This can also give you ideas for an Extended essay. There is a lot of great mathematics out there!

Exam hint

Although we would encourage you to think of mathematics as more than just learning in order to pass an examination, there are some common errors it is useful for you to be aware of. If there is a common pitfall we will try to highlight it in these boxes. We also point out where graphical calculators can be used effectively to simplify a question or speed up your work.

EXAM HINT

Fast forward / rewind

Mathematics is all about making links. You might be interested to see how something you have just learned will be used elsewhere in the course, or you may need to go back and remind yourself of a previous topic. These boxes indicate connections with other sections of the book to help you find your way around.

How to use the questions

The colour-coding

The questions are colour-coded to distinguish between the levels.

Black questions are drill questions. They help you practise the methods described in the book, but they are usually not structured like the questions in the examination. This does not mean they are easy, some of them are quite tough.

Each differently numbered drill question tests a different skill. Lettered subparts of a question are of increasing difficulty. Within each lettered part there may be multiple roman-numeral parts ((i), (ii), ...) , all of which are of a similar difficulty. Unless you want to do lots of practice we would recommend that you only do one roman-numeral part and then check your answer. If you have made a mistake then you may want to think about what went wrong before you try any more. Otherwise move on to the next lettered part.

Green questions are examination-style questions which should be accessible to students on the path to getting a grade 3 or 4.

Blue questions are harder examination-style questions. If you are aiming for a grade 5 or 6 you should be able to make significant progress through most of these.

Red questions are at the very top end of difficulty in the examinations. If you can do these then you are likely to be on course for a grade 7.

Gold questions are a type that are *not* set in the examination, but are designed to provoke thinking and discussion in order to help you to a better understanding of a particular concept.

At the end of each chapter you will see longer questions typical of the second section of International Baccalaureate® examinations. These follow the same colour-coding scheme.

Of course, these are just **guidelines**. If you are aiming for a grade 6, do not be surprised if you find a green question you cannot do. People are never equally good at all areas of the syllabus. Equally, if you can do all the red questions that does not guarantee you will get a grade 7; after all, in the examination you have to deal with time pressure and examination stress!

These questions are graded relative to our experience of the final examination, so when you first start the course you will find all the questions relatively hard, but by the end of the course they should seem more straightforward. Do not get intimidated!

We hope you find the Sets, Relations and Groups Option an interesting and enriching course. You might also find it quite challenging, but do not get intimidated, frequently topics only make sense after lots of revision and practice. Persevere and you will succeed.

The author team.

Introduction

In this Option you will learn:

- about sets and notation for their description, size, exclusions and subsets
- about operations on sets and the qualities of closure, associativity, commutativity and distributivity for operations
- the concept of identity and inverse elements for a given operation
- set operations of union, intersection, set difference and symmetric difference, and the interactions between them
- the Cartesian product of two sets and how to interpret ordered pairs
- about relations as subsets of Cartesian products, the concepts of domain and range for a relation and the qualities of reflexivity, symmetry and transitivity for relations
- equivalence relations, equivalence classes and the specific example of numerical congruence modulo n as an equivalence relation on integers
- about functions as restricted examples of relations, the concepts of domain, range and codomain for a function and the qualities of injectivity, surjectivity and bijectivity for functions
- composition of functions, the inverse of a bijective function and how to determine these
- the four axioms of a group and the additional requirement for an Abelian group
- about cyclic groups and their generator elements
- Lagrange's Theorem and its corollaries which show how the order of a group can be used to provide information on the orders of elements and subgroups
- about the structures of small groups; specifically cyclic groups, the Klein 4-group and the dihedral group D_3
- examples of groups: Functions, symmetries of plane figures and permutations
- about homomorphisms as functions between groups of identical structure which preserve operations; isomorphisms as bijective homomorphisms.

Introductory problem

An automated shuffling machine splits a deck of n cards in half; if n is odd it leaves the extra card in the lower half. It then inverts the lower half and exactly interleaves the two, so that an ordered deck of cards labelled 1, 2, 3, ..., n would, after one shuffle, be in the order n, 1, $(n-1)$, 2, $(n-2)$, 3, ... The machine is used on a deck of seven cards.

After how many shuffles would the deck have returned to its original order?

Would it be possible to use the machine to exactly reverse a deck of n cards? If so, for what values of n?

In your mathematical studies so far you have learned to take a great many arithmetic rules for granted. Many of these may not have been justified in a meaningful way other than 'this is just how it works'.

Why, for example, is it logical that $0! = 1$?

Why is it that when adding or multiplying numbers, the order of values is irrelevant (so that $a + b = b + a$ and $a \times b = b \times a$) while for division and subtraction, reversal of order fundamentally alters the result? You also know that in vector multiplication, order does not affect the result of a scalar product, but does impact upon the vector product.

Is there some classification that separates those operations which are or are not affected in this way? In group theory, we consider mathematical operations in a more abstract way and establish rules and connections between different types of operation. In doing so, it is possible to find links between different types of problem and to transfer conclusions from one branch of mathematics to another.

1 Preliminaries: Proof by contradiction

In this chapter you will learn:

- about different types of proof used in mathematics
- how and when to use proof by contradiction.

Throughout the course you will have encountered derivations of new results: Double-angled identities, the derivative of x^2 and the quadratic formula are some examples. Most of these were **direct proofs**, which means that we started from some results we already knew and derived new results by direct calculation. However, there are some mathematical results that cannot be proved in this way. One of the most quoted examples is the proof that $\sqrt{2}$ is an irrational number: since its decimal expansion is infinite, we cannot show that it never repeats!

An alternative approach is to try and show that $\sqrt{2}$ cannot be written as a fraction; but how can you show by direct calculation that something cannot be done? In this situation we need to use an **indirect proof**, where we find some roundabout way of showing that the statement must be true. For example, we could try to see what would happen if $\sqrt{2}$ could be written as a fraction and hope that this leads to an impossible conclusion; this is called **proof by contradiction**.

You should have already met one example of indirect proof, **proof by induction**, which is used to show that a given statement is true for all integers above a certain starting value. This involves showing that the statement is true for the starting number, and that having proved it for some number we can also prove it for the next one; we can then conclude that the statement *can be proved* for all integers, even if we have only directly proved it for the first one.

Here is another example. Suppose that we have an odd square number n^2 and we want to prove that n must also be an odd number. It is not really obvious how to start. We could try taking the square root of n^2, but we don't know whether this produces an odd number (remember, this is what we are trying to prove!). However, thinking about what would happen if n was *not* an odd number allows us to do some calculations: If n was not odd it would be even, and the product of two even numbers is also even, so n^2 would be even. But we were told that n^2 was odd, so this situation is impossible! We can therefore conclude that n must be odd. This way of reasoning is summarised below.

Can a mathematical statement be true before it has been proved?

Proof by contradiction is a special case of a more general form of argument, called *reductio ad absurdum*, in which a proposition is disproved by showing that its truth would lead to an impossible conclusion. This type of argument relies on the *law of excluded middle*, which states that either a proposition or its negation must be true.

Proof by contradiction was already used by Euclid around 300 BCE. One of the most famous examples was his proof that there are infinitely many prime numbers. Although it has been a widely used tool in mathematics since then, its validity has been disputed by some, most notably by the 20th Century Dutch mathematician and philosopher L.E.J. Brouwer.

KEY POINT 1.1

Proof by contradiction

You can prove that a statement is true by showing that if the opposite were true, it would contradict some of your assumptions (or something else you already know to be true).

We shall now use proof by contradiction to show that $\sqrt{2}$ is an irrational number. Remember that the definition of an irrational number is that it cannot be written in the form $\frac{p}{q}$, where p and q are integers. It is difficult (if not impossible) to express the fact that a number is not of a certain form using an equation. Here, proof by contradiction is a really useful tool: start by assuming that $\sqrt{2}$ is of the form $\frac{p}{q}$.

Worked example 1.1

Prove that $\sqrt{2}$ cannot be written in the form $\frac{p}{q}$, where $p, q \in \mathbb{Z}$.

Try proof by contradiction: Start by writing $\sqrt{2}$ as a fraction and show that this leads to impossible consequences

> Suppose that $\sqrt{2} = \frac{p}{q}$ with $p, q \in \mathbb{Z}$,

The same fraction can be written in several ways $\left(\text{e.g. } \frac{1}{2} = \frac{3}{6} = \frac{5}{10}\right)$ so we should specify which one we are using

> and that the fraction is in its simplest form so that p and q have no common factors.

We can now do some calculations

> Then $\frac{p^2}{q^2} = 2$ (squaring both sides), so $p^2 = 2q^2$.

Looking for common factors is useful in solving problems involving integers

> This means that p^2 is even, so p must also be even: $p = 2r$.
> Then
> $$(2r)^2 = 2q^2$$
> $$\Rightarrow 4r^2 = 2q^2$$
> $$\Rightarrow 2r^2 = q^2$$
> so q^2 is even and therefore q is also even.

We have reached a contradiction, as we assumed that p and q had no common factors

> Hence p and q have common factor 2, which is a contradiction.
> So $\sqrt{2}$ cannot be written as $\frac{p}{q}$.

We shall use proof by contradiction to prove several results in this option. The exercise below is intended to give you some practice in writing up this type of proof, but does not represent typical examination questions.

One of the most fascinating examples of proof by contradiction is Cantor's diagonal proof, which shows that it is impossible to put all real numbers into an (infinite) list.

Exercise 1A

1. Prove that if n^2 is an even integer then n is also an even integer.

2. Show that there are no positive integers x and y such that $x^2 - y^2 = 1$.

3. Prove that $\log_2 5$ is an irrational number.

4. Prove that there is no largest even integer.

5. The mean age of five students is 18. Show that at least one of them must be at least 18 years old.

6. Show that the sum of a rational and an irrational number is irrational.

7. Prove the converse of Pythagoras' theorem: If a, b, c are the sides of a triangle and $a^2 + b^2 = c^2$, then $\hat{C} = 90°$.

8. (a) Use your calculator to show that the equation $x^3 + x + 1 = 0$ has one real root, and find this root correct to 3 significant figures.

   (b) Prove that this root is irrational.

In this chapter you will learn:

- what defines a set
- about operations and their properties
- to use Cayley tables for results of operations
- to use rules for operations on sets
- about set algebra
- about the interaction of set union and intersection: De Morgan's laws.

2 Sets and operations

Since you should have already done some work on sets and Venn diagrams as part of the core syllabus, much of the material in this chapter will be familiar. However, you will see that here we take a slightly different approach as we develop notions of the abstract structure and rules governing sets; the notation is the same, but the use is often more precise.

We shall use this first chapter of the option to familiarise ourselves both with this more structured approach and with the style of proof and working which we shall employ. You will need a clear understanding of the principle of proof by contradiction, which was explained in chapter 1. You may also wish to revise the method of proof by induction that you learned as part of the core syllabus.

2A Defining sets

You should already be familiar with sets and set notation. We shall revise them below, before we apply more formal logic in this option.

A set is a well-defined collection of items; items in a set are referred to as the elements (also sometimes called members) of the set.

The general notation to describe a set by listing its elements is to use braces { } and comma separation. Order is not relevant (though it is useful to list elements in a standard order) and each different element is listed only once.

For example, we could define the sets A, B and C by:

$$A = \{1,2,3,4,5\}$$
$$B = \{1,3,5,2,4\}$$
$$C = \{5,4,3,2,1\}$$

Since all contain the same elements, they are equal, each being the set of integers between 1 and 5 inclusive. The order given for A is, of course, the one usually used.

The symbol $\in$ indicates membership of a particular set, while $\notin$ indicates that an item is not an element of a set. For example:

$$1 \in \{1, 2, 3, 4, 5\}$$
$$6 \notin \{1, 2, 3, 4, 5\}$$

Rather than listing all elements exhaustively, we can also define a set by description:

- {colours in the US flag} would indicate the set consisting of the colours red, white and blue

- {factors of 6} is the set containing the values 1, 2, 3 and 6.

Alternatively, we can define a set by referring to a predefined set and then imposing restrictions. The restrictions are listed after a colon or vertical bar, using a structure called 'set builder notation'. Using the set $A = \{1, 2, 3, 4, 5\}$, $\{x \in A : x$ is not a factor of $6\}$ means 'the set of all elements x in A such that x is not a factor of 6', that is $\{4, 5\}$.

$\{x \in A \mid x^2 \in A\}$ means 'the set of elements x of A such that x^2 is an element of A', that is $\{1, 2\}$.

You may see either a colon or a vertical bar used in the IB exam questions and in other texts, but in this option a vertical bar will always be used (for consistency).

Exclusions from a set can also be listed, using the slash symbol:

$$A \setminus \{1, 3\}$$

means 'all elements of set A, excluding values 1 and 3', that is $\{2, 4, 5\}$.

Enumerating a set

A set with a finite number of elements is termed a 'finite set'. The number of elements of a set A is denoted $n(A)$ or $|A|$, and referred to as the **power**, **size** or **cardinality** of set A. A set with an infinite number of elements is termed an 'infinite set'.

Standard number sets

You should already be familiar with several standard number sets, all of which are infinite:

$\mathbb{N}$	represents the set of all Natural numbers	$\mathbb{N} = \{0, 1, 2, 3, \ldots\}$
$\mathbb{Z}$	represents the set of all Integers	$\mathbb{Z} = \{0, \pm 1, \pm 2, \pm 3, \ldots\}$
$\mathbb{Q}$	represents the set of all Rational numbers	$\mathbb{Q} = \left\{ \dfrac{p}{q} \mid p \in \mathbb{Z}, q \in \mathbb{Z} \setminus \{0\} \right\}$
$\mathbb{R}$	represents the set of all Real numbers	
$\mathbb{C}$	represents the set of all Complex numbers	$\mathbb{C} = \{x + iy \mid x, y \in \mathbb{R}\}$

Some texts will define $\mathbb{N}$ without the element zero, but the definition given above is that adopted by the IB.

The set of real numbers cannot easily be written as a list or structure, but can be considered as the set of all values that can be expressed as either terminating or non-terminating decimals.

The Venn diagram below illustrates that each of the five number sets lies entirely within the set(s) below it in the table.

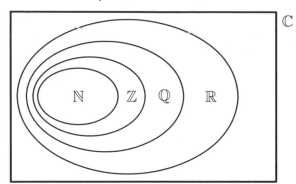

We use a superscript $^+$ to indicate the positive values within a set (so that $\mathbb{Z}^+ = \{x \in \mathbb{Z} \mid x > 0\}$). You may see in other texts * or $^\times$ used to indicate a number set lacking zero (so that $\mathbb{Z} \setminus \{0\}$ could be alternatively written as $\mathbb{Z}^*$ or $\mathbb{Z}^\times$), but we shall not use this notation.

Remember that we use square brackets to indicate intervals on the real line, so that $\{x \in \mathbb{R} \mid a \le x \le b\}$ can be written as $[a,b]$ and $\{x \in \mathbb{R} \mid a < x < b\}$ is $]a,b[$.

Universal and empty sets

In any given problem involving sets, there will be a limit on which elements are being considered; the set of all these elements is called the **universal set**, denoted as U. The universal set may be explicitly defined or may be implicit from context; for example, if a question relates to the factors of integers, it will be clear that $U = \mathbb{Z}^+$ (or some part of $\mathbb{Z}^+$). Once the universal set is defined, no elements outside the universal set are considered when listing elements of a set. For example, if we define $U = \{x \in \mathbb{Z} \mid 0 \le x < 10\}$ then the set E of all even numbers will be $E = \{0, 2, 4, 6, 8\}$. It is not necessary to repeat that we are only interested in integers between 0 and 9 inclusive.

In a Venn diagram, the universal set is indicated by a rectangle which contains any other sets.

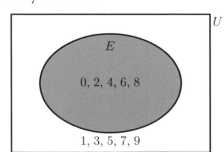

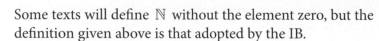

The definition of a universal set given here is that used in the IB; in advanced set theory, universal set has a different meaning, and is used to refer to the 'set containing all sets' (including itself). This concept gives rise to 'Russell's paradox', a source of great dissent in the early years of set theory.

A set containing no elements at all is termed the 'empty set', and is given by the symbol $\varnothing$:

$$\varnothing = \{\,\}$$

Complementary sets

Once the universal set is established, every set A has a **complement** set A' within U, containing all values in U which are not present in A.

$$A' = U \setminus A$$

Necessarily, all elements of U lie exclusively either in A or in A', but never in both.

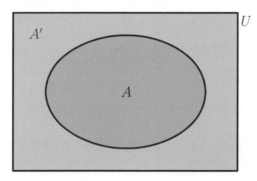

A' is also sometimes termed the **absolute complement** to distinguish it from the concept of 'relative complement', which we shall meet in Section 2C of this Option.

Subsets

If all the elements of a set A are also elements of a set B, then A is termed a **subset** of B and B is a **superset** of A, written $A \subseteq B$ and $B \supseteq A$, respectively.

If $A \subseteq B$ and there are elements of B which are not present in A, then A is a *proper subset* of B, written $A \subset B$.

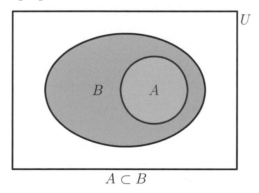

$$A \subset B$$

Thus:

$$\{1,2,3\} \subset \{1,2,3,4,5\}$$

$$\{1,2,3\} \subseteq \{1,2,3,4,5\}$$

$$\{1,2,3\} \subseteq \{1,2,3\}$$

But:

$$\{1,2,3\} \not\subset \{1,2,3\}$$

$$\{1,2,3\} \not\subseteq \{1,3,5\}$$

Clearly for any two sets A and B, if each is a subset of the other then neither contains any element missing from the other, and hence they must be equal.

$A \subseteq B$ and $B \subseteq A$ if and only if $A = B$

This fact is frequently used to prove equality of sets. By establishing that any element of B must be an element of A so that $B \subseteq A$, and also that any element of A must be an element of B so that $A \subseteq B$, we can demonstrate that A and B are equal.

The empty set is technically a subset of every set. For any set C, $\varnothing$ fulfils the rule 'every element of $\varnothing$ is an element in C'. Similarly, set C is also considered a subset of itself.

Both $\varnothing$ and C itself are termed 'trivial subsets' of C.

So far, we have considered examples of sets whose elements are colours and numbers. It is important to realise that the elements of a set can be any type of object. Importantly, and very usefully, we can consider sets whose elements are also sets.

EXAM HINT

If asked to find a subset in an examination question, you should give a proper subset, and not the empty set!

Worked example 2.1

The set of all possible subsets of a set A is called the power set of A, denoted $\mathcal{P}(A)$.

Set $A = \{1,2,3\}$. List the elements of $\mathcal{P}(A)$.

List the elements systematically by size. Don't forget the two trivial subsets

$\mathcal{P}(A) = \{\varnothing, \{1\}, \{2\}, \{3\}, \{1,2\}, \{1,3\}, \{2,3\}, \{1,2,3\}\}$

Notice that in Worked example 2.1, we see the empty set $\varnothing$ shown as an element of $\mathcal{P}(A)$. Is it a useful concept to talk about sets containing empty sets?

Exercise 2A

1. List the elements of the sets:
   (a) (i) $\{a,b,c,d\}$
       (ii) $\{2,4,6,8\}$
   (b) (i) {vowels in the English alphabet}
       (ii) {single digit prime numbers}
   (c) (i) $\{x \in \mathbb{N} \mid x < 5\}$
       (ii) $\{x \in \mathbb{R} \mid x^2 = 4\}$

(d) (i) $\{x \in \mathbb{Z} \mid 3x < x^2 < 20\}$

    (ii) $\{z \in \mathbb{C} \mid z^5 = z\}$

(e) (i) $\{2n+1 \mid n \in \mathbb{N}, n \le 4\}$

    (ii) $\{3x \mid x \in \mathbb{Z}, |x| < 3\}$

2. State the cardinality of the following sets:

  (a) (i) $\{a,b,c,d\}$

     (ii) $\{3,2\}$

  (b) (i) $\varnothing$

     (ii) $\{\varnothing\}$

  (c) (i) {pitches in a chromatic scale}

     (ii) {US states}

  (d) (i) $\{x \in \mathbb{N} \mid x < 7\}$

     (ii) $\{x \in \mathbb{Z} \mid x < 7\}$

  (e) (i) $\{x \in \mathbb{Z}^+ \mid \mathrm{lcm}(x,6) < 20\}$

     (ii) $\{x \in \mathbb{Z} \mid x^2 - 8 \le |x|\}$

3. For each of the following sets, state if it is a proper subset of:

  (i) $\mathbb{N}$ (ii) $\mathbb{Z}$ (iii) $\mathbb{Q}$ (iv) $\mathbb{R}$

  (a) $\{1,2,3.5\}$

  (b) $\{x : x^2 > -1\}$

  (c) $\{x+1 \mid x \in \mathbb{N}\}$

  (d) $\left\{\dfrac{1}{x} \mid x \in \mathbb{Z} \setminus \{0\}\right\}$

4. For each of the following, state whether $A \subset B, A \supset B$ or $A = B$. If one is a proper subset of the other, give an example of an element *present* in the superset and *absent* from the subset.

  (a) $A = \mathbb{N}, B = \mathbb{Z}$

  (b) $A = \{x^2 \mid x \in \mathbb{N}\}, B = \{x^2 \mid x \in \mathbb{Z}\}$

  (c) $A = \mathbb{R}^+, B = \{q^r \mid q \in \mathbb{Q}^+, r \in \mathbb{Q}\}$

  (d) $A = \varnothing, B = \{\varnothing\}$

5. Using the definition given in Worked example 2.1, for each of the following sets A, write down the power set $\mathcal{P}(A)$:

  (a) $A = \{0,1\}$

  (b) $A = \{a,b,c,d\}$

6. Using the definition given in Worked example 2.1, prove that for any finite set A for which $n(A) = k$, $n(\mathcal{P}(A)) = 2^k$.

2B Operations

A **binary operation** on a set is a well-defined rule for combining two elements of the set to produce a unique result, which may or may not also be an element of the set.

You already know some operations from basic arithmetic, such as addition, subtraction, multiplication, division and exponentiation. We use the symbols $+, -, \times, \div$ and $\wedge$ respectively to indicate each of these operations. When applying an operation to two elements x and y of our number set, we write the operation symbol between its two input values (called operands or arguments):

$$x + y$$

$$x - y$$

$$x \times y$$

$$x \div y$$

$$x \wedge y$$

So far this is familiar, although we are more accustomed to seeing $x \wedge y$ written as x^y.

When considering operations in the abstract, we shall generally use non-specific symbols such as $*$ and $\circ$ to represent an operation, and define the rules of the operation separately. Where an operation is closely related to one of the standard arithmetic operations, we frequently denote the operation by circling the arithmetic symbol: for example $\oplus$ and $\otimes$.

You know some operations which use only one element (unary operations, such as 'factorial'). There are also operations taking three or more elements; study of these does not come within the syllabus for this option, though you should consider how the rules and considerations given below might be adapted for unary or ternary (three element) operations.

For simplicity we shall from now on refer only to 'operations' rather than 'binary operations'.

Closure

Let us consider the five operations given above when used in the set $\mathbb{Z}^+$. We notice that, although $x * y \in \mathbb{Z}^+$ for all $x, y \in \mathbb{Z}^+$ when $*$ represents addition, the same is not true when $*$ represents subtraction; for example, $2 - 3 \notin \mathbb{Z}^+$. In fact, we can only be fully confident that $x * y$ will always be an element of $\mathbb{Z}^+$ for addition, multiplication and exponentiation.

We describe this formally by saying:

'$\mathbb{Z}^+$ is closed under addition, multiplication or exponentiation.'

'$\mathbb{Z}^+$ is not closed under subtraction or division.'

> For an operation ∗ on a set S, S is said to be **closed** under ∗
> if $x * y \in S$ for all $x, y \in S$.

Note that the closure property requires this to hold for *all*
elements. It only takes a single exception for closure to be lost.

Worked example 2.2

Which of the following sets is closed under the given operation?

(a) $\mathbb{Z}$ under multiplication ($\times$)

(b) $\mathbb{R}$ under division ($\div$)

(c) $\mathbb{Q} \setminus \{0\}$ under division ($\div$)

(d) $\mathbb{Q}^+$ under exponentiation ($\wedge$)

(e) $\mathbb{Z}$ under subtraction ($-$)

(f) $\{-1, 0, 1\}$ under multiplication ($\times$)

Establish that $x * y \in S$ for all $x, y \in S$
or give a counter-example to prove
non-closure

(a) Closed: the product of two integers is
also an integer

(b) Not closed: $a \div 0 \notin \mathbb{R}$ for all $a \in \mathbb{R}$

(c) Closed: the ratio of any two non-zero rational
values is also a non-zero rational value

(d) Not closed: for example, $2 \wedge \dfrac{1}{2} \notin \mathbb{Q}^+$

(e) Closed: the difference of two integers is
also an integer

(f) Closed: the product table for this three-
element set under multiplication is

$\times$	-1	0	1
-1	1	0	-1
0	0	0	0
1	-1	0	1

Notice that the most direct approach to answering part (f) of
Worked example 2.2 was to show all the possible results of
the operation in a table as there was a (very small) finite set of
elements. This is an example of a '**Cayley table**', named after
mathematician Arthur Cayley.

For an operation $*$ on a finite set $S = \{a_1, a_2, \ldots, a_n\}$, the Cayley table is laid out as follows:

$*$	a_1	a_2	$\ldots$	a_n
a_1	$a_1 * a_1$	$a_1 * a_2$	$\ldots$	$a_1 * a_n$
a_2	$a_2 * a_1$	$a_2 * a_2$	$\ldots$	$a_2 * a_n$
$\ldots$	$\ldots$	$\ldots$	$\ldots$	$\ldots$
a_n	$a_n * a_1$	$a_n * a_2$	$\ldots$	$a_n * a_n$

Each cell of the grid is the result of the operation taking its first operand from the **row** title and its second operand from the column title.

Worked example 2.3

Operators $*$ and $\circ$ are defined on the set $S = \{0,1,2,3\}$ by

$$a * b = a^{1+b} - b^{1+a} \text{ and } a \circ b = \frac{1}{2}(a - 2b + |2b - a|).$$

Draw out the Cayley tables for $*$ on S and $\circ$ on S, and state whether each is closed.

For each cell, combine the row title with the column title according to the formula given. So, for example
$$0 * 2 = 0^{1+2} - 2^{1+0} = 0 - 2 = -2$$

$*$	0	1	2	3
0			-2	
1				
2				
3				

Complete the Cayley table. The set is closed under the operation if all elements in the cells of the table are elements of the original set

$*$	0	1	2	3
0	0	-1	-2	-3
1	1	0	-3	-8
2	2	3	0	-11
3	3	8	11	0

A single example is sufficient to demonstrate an operation is not closed

As shown in the table, $*$ is not closed on S; for example, $0, 1 \in S$ but $0 * 1 \notin S$

$\circ$	0	1	2	3
0	0	0	0	0
1	1	0	0	0
2	2	0	0	0
3	3	1	0	0

As shown in the table, $\circ$ is closed on S, since $a \circ b \in S$ for all $a, b \in S$

Commutativity

We know that for the operations addition and multiplication, the order of the two operands makes no difference to the result, whether we are using elements from $\mathbb{N}$, $\mathbb{Z}$, $\mathbb{Q}$, $\mathbb{R}$ or $\mathbb{C}$.

$x + y = y + x$ for all x, y

$x \times y = y \times x$ for all x, y

Subtraction, division and exponentiation do not have this property, since the order cannot be reversed for *every* pair of elements in the number set.

Any operation for which the order of operands chosen makes no difference to the result is said to be **commutative** in that set.

KEY POINT 2.4

An operation $*$ on a set S is said to be commutative in S if

$x * y = y * x$ for all $x, y \in S$.

If the row and column titles of a Cayley table are laid out in the same order then, for a commutative operation, that table will be symmetrical about the leading diagonal.

Worked example 2.4

Which of the following operations is commutative for the given set?

(a) $x * y$ is defined in $\mathbb{Z}$ as $x * y = xy + x + y$

(b) $x \Diamond y$ is defined in $\mathbb{R}$ as $x \Diamond y = 2^x - 2^y$

(c) $x \ddagger y$ is defined in $\{1, 2, 3, 4, 5\}$ as $x \ddagger y = 2 \times \min(x, y) - \max(x, y)$

Demonstrate $x * y = y * x$ or find a counter-example

(a) Commutative
$$x * y = xy + x + y$$
$$= yx + y + x$$
$$= y * x$$

Demonstrate $x \Diamond y = y \Diamond x$ or find a counter-example

(b) Not commutative. For example,
$$2 \Diamond 1 = 2^2 - 2^1 = 2$$
$$1 \Diamond 2 = 2^1 - 2^2 = -2$$

Demonstrate $x \ddagger y = y \ddagger x$ or find a counter-example

(c) Commutative
$$x \ddagger y = 2\min(x, y) - \max(x, y)$$
$$= 2\min(y, x) - \max(y, x)$$
$$= y \ddagger x$$

Identity element

An **identity element** for a given operation has the property that it leaves unchanged every other element in the given set under the operation. The identity element for an arbitrary operation is usually represented by the letter e. (Note that this is different from the real constant, $e = 2.718...$)

KEY POINT 2.5

> For an operation $*$ on a set S, an element e is said to be the identity element if it is both a left-identity and a right-identity for the operation in S:
>
> $e * x = x * e = x$ for all $x \in S$
>
> The row of the identity element e in the Cayley table will match the title row, and the column of e will match the title column.

Not every operation on a set will have an identity element within the set, and some operations may not have an identity element at all.

EXAM HINT

If the operation is not commutative, we must check both that $e * x = x$ and also that $x * e = x$ for all x. For an operation $*$ on a set S, an element $e_L \in S$ is said to be a left-identity element if $e_L * x = x$ for all $x \in S$. For an operation $*$ on a set S, an element $e_R \in S$ is said to be a right-identity element if $x * e_R = x$ for all $x \in S$. It is perfectly possible for an operation to have several left-identity elements and right-identity elements, but there can only be one two-sided identity element.

Worked example 2.5

Prove that an operation $*$ in a set S can have at most one identity element.

Proof by contradiction: Suppose that there are two such elements	Suppose $e_1, e_2 \in S$ are both identity elements for $*$ in S
Demonstrate logically that they must be exactly equal	Then $e_1 * e_2 = e_1$ (1) because e_2 is an identity and $e_1 * e_2 = e_2$ (2) because e_1 is an identity $\Rightarrow e_1 = e_2$ (from (1) and (2)) $\therefore$ There can never be two distinct identity elements for an operation in a given set.

Worked example 2.6

For each of the following operations, determine the identity element, if there is one, within the given set.

(a)   Multiplication in $\mathbb{R}$

(b)   Addition in $\mathbb{Z}$

(c) $\dagger$ in $\{3,4,5,6,7\}$ where $\dagger$ is given by $x \dagger y = \max(x, y)$

(d) $*$ in $\mathbb{Q}$ where $*$ is given by $x * y = y$

Find an identity or demonstrate that no such element can exist

(a) $e = 1$

$1 \times x = x \times 1 = x$ for all $x \in \mathbb{R}$

(b) $e = 0$

$0 + x = x + 0 = x$ for all $x \in \mathbb{Z}$

(c) $e = 3$

Since $x \geq 3$ for all $x \in \{3,4,5,6,7\}$,

$\Rightarrow 3 \dagger x = x \dagger 3 = x$ for all $x \in \{3,4,5,6,7\}$

(d) No identity element

Every element in the set is a left-identity, but there is no right-identity, and hence no identity element.

Proof by contradiction:

Suppose there is an identity element e.

There are at least two elements in $\mathbb{Q}$; hence there exists an element $a \in \mathbb{Q}, a \neq e$

$a * e = e$ by the definition of $*$

$\Rightarrow a * e \neq a$ since $e \neq a$

This contradicts the right-identity requirement on e.

There is no identity element

Inverse elements

If a given operation $*$ in a set S has an identity, then we can also introduce the concept of inverse elements.

KEY POINT 2.6

> For an operation $*$ on a set S with identity e, an element $y \in S$ is said to be the inverse of $x \in S$ if $x * y = y * x = e$.
>
> In such a case, y may be written as x^{-1}.

We must take care. We are now considering abstract operations; the superscript '−1' should not be interpreted as an exponent in the normal arithmetic sense.

 You have already met superscripts which are not arithmetic components. Compare how you interpret the −1 in 5^{-1} and in $\sin^{-1}x$

Take for example the set $\mathbb{Z}$ under addition. As demonstrated in Worked example 2.6, the identity for addition (called the additive identity) is 0.

So for a to be the inverse of 2, we require that $2 + a = a + 2 = 0$.

Hence, under the operation addition in $\mathbb{Z}$, $2^{-1} = -2$, a statement that in other contexts would seem utterly false!

More generally, in $\mathbb{Z}$ under addition, $x^{-1} = -x$ for all $x \in \mathbb{Z}$.

Not all elements need have an inverse within the set.

For example, in $\mathbb{R}$ under multiplication, the identity element is 1 (the multiplicative identity) so for every element $x \in \mathbb{R}$ with $x \neq 0$, $x^{-1} = \dfrac{1}{x}$.

However, the element 0 has no inverse, as there is no element in $\mathbb{R}$ whose product with 0 is 1.

Our starting point was familiar arithmetic operations, from which we generalised and made observations on more abstract operations. Which then is more fundamental, the familiar or the abstract?

Worked example 2.7

(a) Find the inverse, if it exists, of 3 in $\mathbb{Q}$ under multiplication.

(b) Find the inverse, if it exists, of 7 in $\mathbb{N}$ under $\dagger$, where $\dagger$ is given by $x \dagger y = \max(x, y)$.

(c) Find the inverse of x in $\mathbb{N}$ under $*$, where $*$ is given by $x * y = |x - y|$.

(d) Find the inverse of x in $\mathbb{R}$ under $*$, where $*$ is given by $x * y = xy + x + y$ and state which values of x have no inverse under $*$.

First find the identity element for the operation. Standard identities (multiplicative and additive) may be quoted. Others should be established	(a) Multiplicative identity $e = 1$
State and prove an inverse	$\dfrac{1}{3} \times 3 = 3 \times \dfrac{1}{3} = e$ $\therefore 3^{-1} = \dfrac{1}{3}$
Find the identity element for the operation	(b) $\max(x, 0) = \max(0, x) = x$ for all $x \in \mathbb{N}$ $\Rightarrow e = 0$
Either state and prove an inverse, or demonstrate rigorously the absence of any possible inverse	$\max(x, 7) \geq 7$ for all $x \in \mathbb{N}$ $\therefore$ there is no element $x \in \mathbb{N}$ such that $\max(x, 7) = 0$ there is no inverse for the element 7
	(c) $x * 0 = 0 * x = x$ for all $x \in \mathbb{N}$ $\Rightarrow e = 0$ Let $y = x^{-1}$ under $*$ $\Rightarrow x * y = y * x = 0$ $\Rightarrow |x - y| = 0$ $\Rightarrow y = x$ $\therefore x^{-1} = x$ for all $x \in \mathbb{N}$

continued . . .

(d) $x * 0 = 0 * x = x$ for all $x \in \mathbb{R}$
$\Rightarrow e = 0$

Let $y = x^{-1}$ under $*$
$\Rightarrow x * y = y * x = 0$
$\Rightarrow xy + x + y = 0$
$\Rightarrow y(x+1) = -x$

$\Rightarrow y = -\dfrac{x}{x+1}$ when $x \neq -1$

Since no such element exists in $\mathbb{R}$ when $x = -1$,
every element except -1 has an inverse under $*$

Notice that in Worked example 2.7c, we found that every element was equal to its own inverse; that is, every element in the set is 'self-inverse'.

KEY POINT 2.7

> For an operation $*$ on a set S with identity e, an element $x \in S$ is said to be **self-inverse** if $x * x = e$.

Associativity

Consider adding three numbers together:

$$4 + 3 + 1$$

We have two operations to perform (both addition). Does it matter which we choose first? In other words, will we get a different answers from $(4+3)+1$ and $4+(3+1)$?

We know that the answer is no, and so we are quite happy to write the original expression using no brackets at all.

However, in the case of subtraction, we do get different results from $(4-3)-1$ and $4-(3-1)$.

We say that an operation applied repeatedly in this way is **associative** if the position of parentheses makes no difference and 'not associative' if parentheses are significant.

Addition is associative in $\mathbb{R}$, and we can simply drop the parentheses and write:

$$x + y + z$$

when adding three elements together.

Subtraction is not associative in $\mathbb{R}$, because parentheses are required to specify which calculation is to be performed first.

KEY POINT 2.8

> An operation $*$ on a set S is said to be associative in S if and only if $x * (y * z) = (x * y) * z$ for all $x, y, z \in S$.

Worked example 2.8

Which of the following operations is associative in the given set?

(a) $x * y$ is defined in $\mathbb{Z}$ as $x * y = xy + x + y$

(b) $x \diamond y$ is defined in $\mathbb{R}$ as $x \diamond y = 2^x - 2^y$

(c) $x \ddagger y$ is defined in $\{1, 2, 3, 4, 5\}$ as $x \ddagger y = 2 \times \min(x, y) - \max(x, y)$

Demonstrate $x * (y * z) = (x * y) * z$ or find a counter-example	(a) Associative

$$x * (y * z) = x * (yz + y + z)$$
$$= x(yz + y + z) + x + (yz + y + z)$$
$$= xyz + xy + xz + yz + x + y + z$$
$$= (xy + x + y)z + (xy + x + y) + z$$
$$= (xy + x + y) * z$$
$$= (x * y) * z$$

Demonstrate $x \diamond (y \diamond z) = (x \diamond y) \diamond z$ or find a counter-example	(b) Not associative: for example,

$$1 \diamond (2 \diamond 3) = 2^1 - (2^2 - 2^3)$$
$$= 2 - (-4)$$
$$= 6$$
$$(1 \diamond 2) \diamond 3 = (2^1 - 2^2) - 2^3$$
$$= -2 - 8$$
$$= -10$$

Demonstrate $x \ddagger (y \ddagger z) = (x \ddagger y) \ddagger z$ or find a counter-example	(c) Not associative: for example,

$$1 \ddagger (5 \ddagger 5) = 1 \ddagger (2\min(5, 5) - \max(5, 5))$$
$$= -1 \ddagger 5$$
$$= -3$$
$$(1 \ddagger 5) \ddagger 5 = (2\min(1, 5) - \max(1, 5)) \ddagger 5$$
$$= -3 \ddagger 5$$
$$= -11$$

If an operation is associative, the position of brackets makes no difference to the end result. We can, for simplicity, not write them at all:

$$x * (y * z) = (x * y) * z = x * y * z$$

In particular, it is convenient to use the shorthand form

$$x * x = x^2$$
$$x * x * x = x^3$$
$$\underbrace{x * x * x * \ldots * x}_{n \text{ times}} = x^n$$

Be aware that the indices $\square^2$, $\square^3$ and $\square^n$ used here are not necessarily the same as exponents in arithmetic, which specifically indicate repeated applications of multiplication.

However, the following familiar rules of exponents do still hold.

KEY POINT 2.9

> For an associative operation $*$ acting on a set S with $x, y \in S$ and for any positive integers m and n:
>
> $$x^m * x^n = x^{m+n}$$
>
> $$\left(x^m\right)^n = x^{mn}$$
>
> If the inverse element x^{-1} exists:
>
> $$x^{-n} = \left(x^n\right)^{-1}$$
>
> However, only if $*$ is commutative can we assert that:
>
> $$x^n * y^n = \left(x * y\right)^n$$

Finally we can consider the interaction of two different operations.

Distributivity

Put simply, this is the quality which allows us to expand brackets. More formally:

KEY POINT 2.10

> For two operations $*$ and $\circ$ acting on a set S, $*$ is **distributive** over $\circ$ if $x * \left(y \circ z\right) = \left(x * y\right) \circ \left(x * z\right)$ for all $x, y, z \in S$.

You are already familiar with an example of this property in basic algebra:

In all standard number sets, multiplication is distributive across addition, since:

$$x \times \left(y + z\right) = \left(x \times y\right) + \left(x \times z\right)$$

However, the reverse is not true. Addition is not distributive across multiplication, since we cannot say that:

$$x + \left(y \times z\right) = \left(x + y\right) \times \left(x + z\right)$$

Worked example 2.9

For which of the following operations is $*$ distributive over $\circ$?

(a) In $\mathbb{R}$: $x * y = x(y+1)$, $x \circ y = x - y$

(b) In $\mathbb{Z}$: $x * y = \max(x, y)$, $x \circ y = x + y$

(c) In $\mathbb{Q}$: $x * y = 3xy$, $x \circ y = 2x - y$

Evaluate $x*(y\circ z)$ and $(x*y)\circ(x*z)$

(a) $x*(y \circ z) = x*(y-z)$

$\qquad = x(y-z+1)$

$\qquad = xy - xz + x$

$(x*y)\circ(x*z) = (xy+x)\circ(xz+x)$

$\qquad = xy + x - (xz+x)$

$\qquad = xy - xz$

Determine whether they are equal for all x,y,z in the given set, giving a counter-example if not

$\Rightarrow x*(y\circ z) = (x*y)\circ(x*z)$ only if $x = 0$

$\Rightarrow *$ is not distributive over $\circ$ in $\mathbb{R}$

Evaluate $x*(y\circ z)$ and $(x*y)\circ(x*z)$

(b) $x*(y \circ z) = x*(y+z)$

$\qquad = \max(x, y+z)$

$(x*y)\circ(x*z) = \max(x,y)\circ\max(x,z)$

$\qquad = \max(x,y) + \max(x,z)$

If you are not sure whether the two are always equal, try some numbers. Determine whether they are equal for all x,y,z in the given set, giving a counter-example if not

Take $x = 3, y = 2, z = 1$:

$3*(2\circ 1) = 3$

$(3*2)\circ(3*1) = 3+3 = 6$

$\therefore 3*(2\circ 1) \neq (3*2)\circ(3*1)$

$\Rightarrow *$ is not distributive over $\circ$ in $\mathbb{Z}$

Evaluate $x*(y\circ z)$ and $(x*y)\circ(x*z)$. Determine whether they are equal for all x,y,z in the given set, giving a counter-example if not

(c) $x*(y \circ z) = x*(2y-z)$

$\qquad = 6xy - 3xz$

$(x*y)\circ(x*z) = (3xy)\circ(3xz)$

$\qquad = 6xy - 3xz$

$\therefore x*(y\circ z) = (x*y)\circ(x*z)$ for all $x,y,z \in S$

$\Rightarrow *$ is distributive over $\circ$ in $\mathbb{Q}$

The scalar triple product of three vectors **a**, **b** and **c** is given as **a**•(**b** × **c**). This is an example of a ternary operation as it takes three elements to produce a result. Investigate the properties of the scalar triple product, and consider how the concepts of closure, commutativity and associativity, as defined above for binary operations, might be interpreted for ternary operations.

Exercise 2B

1. Binary operations $*$ and $\circ$ are defined in $\mathbb{R}$ by:

$$x * y = x - y + 3, \ x \circ y = 3 - xy$$

   (a) Find:
   - (i) $3 * 2$
   - (ii) $7 \circ 2$
   - (iii) $-2 * 1$
   - (iv) $-4 \circ 3$

   (b) (i) Show that $*$ has no identity element.

   (ii) Show that $\circ$ is commutative.

   (c) Solve for x:
   - (i) $x * 2 = 6$
   - (ii) $x \circ 2 = 7$

2. State which of the qualities

   (A) closure

   (B) commutativity

   (C) associativity

   apply to each of the following operations:

   (a) $*$ in $\mathbb{Q}$ where $x * y = \dfrac{x + y}{2}$

   (b) $*$ in $\mathbb{Z}$ where $x * y = 3x - 2y$

   (c) $*$ in $\mathbb{R} \setminus \{0\}$ where $x * y = \dfrac{xy}{x + y}$

   (d) $*$ in $\{2^n \,|\, n \in \mathbb{Q}\}$ where $x * y = x + y$

3. Where it exists, state the identity of the following and find the general form of an inverse to element x:

   (a) (i) $\mathbb{R}$ under $*$ where $x * y = x + y + 1$

   (ii) $\mathbb{R}$ under $*$ where $x * y = 2xy$

   (b) (i) The set of non-zero vectors of three-dimensional space under vector product.

   (ii) The set of vectors of three-dimensional space under vector addition.

   (c) (i) $\mathbb{Q}$ under $*$ where $x * y = \dfrac{|y - x|}{1 + xy}$

   (ii) $\mathbb{C} \setminus \{0\}$ under $*$ where $v * w = |v|\operatorname{cis}\big(\arg(w)\big)$

4. Draw the Cayley table, determine closure and identify the identity element (if it exists) for:

   (a) $\{0,1,2,3\}$ under $*$ where $x * y = |xy - x - y|$

   (b) $\{0,2,4,6\}$ under $*$ where $x * y = \dfrac{xy}{4}$

   (c) $\{7,8,9\}$ under $*$ where $x * y = \max(x, y)$

5. Operations $*$ and $\circ$ are defined on a set $S \subseteq \mathbb{Z}$ by:
$$a * b = \max(a-b, b-a)$$
$$a \circ b = ab - a - b + 2$$

(a) Which of the following is true?

(i) $*$ is closed on $\mathbb{Z}$

(ii) $*$ is closed on $\mathbb{N}$

(iii) $\circ$ is closed on $\{0,1,2,3\}$

(iv) $\circ$ is closed on $\mathbb{N}$

(b) Which of the following is true?

(i) $*$ is commutative

(ii) $\circ$ is commutative

(c) Which of the following is true?

(i) $*$ is associative

(ii) $\circ$ is associative

(d) Determine the identity element, if one exists, for:

(i) $*$ in $\mathbb{Z}^+$

(ii) $\circ$ in $\mathbb{Z}$

(e) Determine for which $x \in \mathbb{Z}$ there is an inverse x^{-1} and express x^{-1} in terms of x.

(i) $*$ in $\mathbb{Z}$

(ii) $\circ$ in $\mathbb{Z}$

6. Operations $*$ and $\circ$ are defined on $\mathbb{R}^+$ by:
$$x * y = xy \quad \text{and} \quad x \circ y = y^x$$

Show that $\circ$ is distributive over $*$.

7. For $k \in \mathbb{Z}$, the binary operation $*_k$ is defined for $x, y \in \mathbb{Z}^+$ by:

$$x *_k y = x + y - k$$

Determine whether or not $*_k$ is:

(a) closed

(b) commutative

(c) associative

Find:

(d) the identity element of $*_k$

(e) the subset of $\mathbb{Z}^+$ having an inverse under $*_k$

8. For an operation $*$ on a set A, an absorbing element z is defined as any element such that $a * z = z * a = z$ for all $a \in A$.

(a) Prove that:

(i) There can be at most one absorbing element for an operation $*$.

(ii) An absorbing element can have no inverse under $*$.

(b) Find an absorbing element for:

   (i) $\mathbb{Q}$ under multiplication

   (ii) $\mathbb{Z}^+$ under gcd (greatest common divisor)

   (iii) $\mathbb{R}$ under $\ast$ where $x \ast y = xy - 2x - 2y + 6$

2C Operations on sets

Now we have some general terminology for operations, we can consider the various operations which act upon subsets of U.

Union of sets

$A \cup B$ is the **union** of A and B, a set containing all elements of A and all elements of B; for example

$$\{1,2,3\} \cup \{1,3,5\} = \{1,2,3,5\}$$

Notice that elements 1 and 3 were present in both sets on the left side, but are only listed once in the union because elements are not repeated within a set.

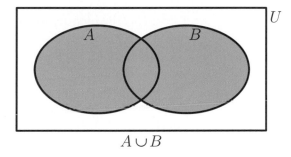

$A \cup B$

Properties of union: for any sets $A, B, C \subseteq U$

$A \cup B = B \cup A$	Union is commutative
$A \cup (B \cup C) = (A \cup B) \cup C$	Union is associative
$A \cup \varnothing = A$	$\varnothing$ is the identity for union
$A \cup A' = U$	The union of complementary sets is U

Intersection of sets

$A \cap B$ is the **intersection** of A and B, a set containing only those elements present in both A and B; for example,

$$\{1,2,3\} \cap \{1,3,5\} = \{1,3\}$$

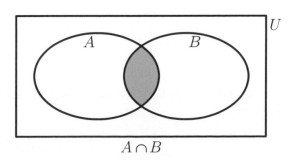

$A \cap B$

Any two sets whose intersection is the empty set are termed **disjoint** sets; for example,

$$\{1,2,3\} \cap \{4,5\} = \varnothing$$

Hence $\{1,2,3\}$ and $\{4,5\}$ are disjoint sets.

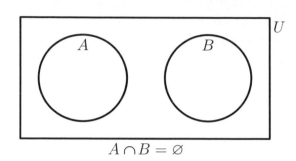

$$A \cap B = \varnothing$$

Properties of intersection: for any sets $A, B, C \subseteq U$

$A \cap B = B \cap A$	Intersection is commutative
$A \cap (B \cap C) = (A \cap B) \cap C$	Intersection is associative
$A \cap U = A$	U is the identity for intersection
$A \cap A' = \varnothing$	Complementary sets are disjoint

Now that we have a clear definition of union and intersection, we can make a formal definition of the idea of a **partition**:

KEY POINT 2.11

The set A is *partitioned* by non-empty subsets $B_1, B_2, \ldots$ if

$\quad B_i \cap B_j = \varnothing$ for any $i \neq j$ (the subsets are disjoint)

$\quad B_1 \cup B_2 \cup \ldots = A$ (the union of all the subsets equals A)

We have already met a very simple example of a partition: A and A' partition U, as illustrated in the diagram for complementary sets in Section 2A.

EXAM HINT

You will often need to quote these rules of distributivity of intersection and union, but will not be expected to prove them algebraically, though you may have to illustrate them using Venn diagrams.

Properties of distributivity for intersection and union: for any sets $A, B, C \subseteq U$,

$A \cap (B \cup C) = (A \cap B) \cup (A \cap C)$	Intersection is distributive over union
$A \cup (B \cap C) = (A \cup B) \cap (A \cup C)$	Union is distributive over intersection

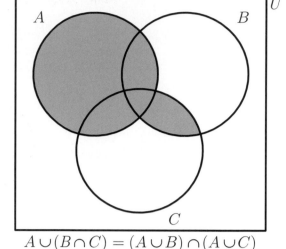

$$A \cap (B \cup C) = (A \cap B) \cup (A \cap C) \qquad A \cup (B \cap C) = (A \cup B) \cap (A \cup C)$$

Set difference

$A \setminus B$ has already been loosely described in Section 2A of this chapter; it is called the relative complement or **set difference** of A and B and can now be formally defined as:

$$A \setminus B = A \cap B'$$

e.g. $\{1,2,3\} \setminus \{1,3,5\} = \{2\}$

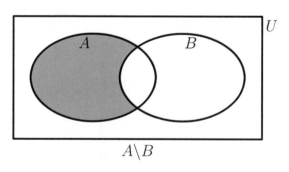

$A \setminus B$

> Some texts may use the alternative notation $A - B$, since we begin with the elements in A and then remove any elements which also appear in B.

Notice that set difference is not commutative: $A \setminus B$ is not equivalent to $B \setminus A$:

$$\text{e.g. } \{1,3,5\} \setminus \{1,2,3\} = \{5\}$$

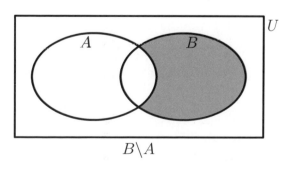

$B \setminus A$

Properties of set difference: for any sets $A, B \subseteq U$

$(A \setminus B) \cap (B \setminus A) = \varnothing$	Reversed set differences are disjoint
$A \setminus A = \varnothing$	Self-difference is the empty set
$A \setminus \varnothing = A$	$\varnothing$ is the right-identity for set difference

Set difference is not generally commutative or associative.

Symmetric difference

$A \triangle B$ is the **symmetric difference** of A and B, and is the set of those elements which are members of exactly one of A and B, but do not lie in their intersection; for example,

$$\{1,2,3\} \triangle \{1,3,5\} = \{2,5\}$$

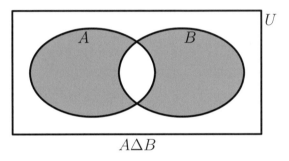

$A \triangle B$

Notice that we could define this either as the union without the intersection,

$$A \triangle B = (A \cup B) \setminus (A \cap B)$$

or as the union of the two relative complements

$$A \triangle B = (A \setminus B) \cup (B / A).$$

Properties of symmetric difference: for any sets $A, B, C \subseteq U$

$A \triangle B = B \triangle A$	Symmetric difference is commutative
$A \triangle (B \triangle C) = (A \triangle B) \triangle C$	Symmetric difference is associative
$A \triangle \varnothing = A$	$\varnothing$ is the identity for symmetric difference
$A \triangle A = \varnothing$	Every set is self-inverse under symmetric difference

Worked example 2.10

$U = \{x \in \mathbb{N} \mid x < 8\}$, $A = \{1,2,3,4,5\}$ and $B = \{1,2,4,6\}$.

List the elements of the following sets:

    (a) A' (b) $A \setminus B$ (c) $A \cup B$

    (d) $A \cap B$ (e) $A \, \Delta \, B$

> It helps to list the elements of the universal set

$U = \{0,1,2,3,4,5,6,7\}$

    (a) $A' = \{0,6,7\}$
    (b) $A \setminus B = \{3,5\}$
    (c) $A \cup B = \{1,2,3,4,5,6\}$
    (d) $A \cap B = \{1,2,4\}$
    (e) $A \, \Delta \, B = \{3,5,6\}$

De Morgan's laws

We have already seen that union and intersection are distributive over each other.

We can also show, using Venn diagrams, that the complement of an intersection is the union of complements, and that the complement of a union is the intersection of complements:

KEY POINT 2.12

De Morgan's laws state that:

$$(A \cup B)' = A' \cap B'$$
$$(A \cap B)' = A' \cup B'$$

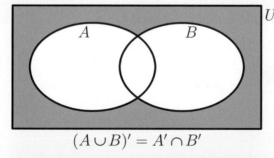

$(A \cup B)' = A' \cap B'$

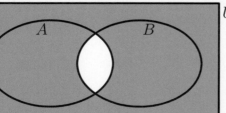

$(A \cap B)' = A' \cup B'$

> **EXAM HINT**
>
> You may be asked for proofs using set algebra. In most cases, you should expect to use either De Morgan's laws or the rules of distributivity of union and intersection, both of which can be quoted. You should never be required to prove De Morgan's laws algebraically.

Worked example 2.11

Prove that $A \setminus (B \cup C) = (A \setminus B) \cap (A \setminus C)$.

Proof that two sets equal each other:
Prove that each is a subset of the other

Take an arbitrary element in the left
hand set and show it must be an
element of the right hand set

Suppose $x \in A \setminus (B \cup C)$
$\Rightarrow x \in A$ and $x \in (B \cup C)'$
$\Rightarrow x \in A$ and $x \in B' \cap C'$ by De Morgan's law
$\Rightarrow x \in A$ and $x \in B'$ and $x \in C'$
$\Rightarrow x \in A \cap B'$ and $x \in A \cap C'$
$\therefore A \setminus (B \cup C) \subseteq (A \setminus B) \cap (A \setminus C)$ (1)

Then repeat, showing that an element of
the RHS must be an element of the LHS

Suppose $x \in (A \setminus B) \cap (A \setminus C)$
$\Rightarrow x \in A \cap B'$ and $x \in A \cap C'$
$\Rightarrow x \in A$ and $x \in B'$ and $x \in C'$
$\Rightarrow x \in A$ and $x \in B' \cap C'$
$\Rightarrow x \in A$ and $x \in (B \cup C)'$ by De Morgan's law
$\therefore (A \setminus B) \cap (A \setminus C) \subseteq A \setminus (B \cup C)$ (2)

Having established each is a subset of
the other, we can conclude the sets are
equal

(1) & (2)
$\Rightarrow A \setminus (B \cup C) = (A \setminus B) \cap (A \setminus C)$

Worked example 2.12

Prove that for any sets A and B, $A \cup B = A \cap B$ if and only if $A = B$.

Proving if and only if: Prove each
direction separately

Proof that $A \cup B = A \cap B \Rightarrow A = B$:

Proof that two sets equal each other:
Prove that each is a subset of the
other

Assume $A \cup B = A \cap B$

continued . . .

Take an arbitrary element in the left
hand set and show it must be an
element of the right hand set, then do
the equivalent steps to show that an
element of the right hand set must be an
element of the left hand set

Take an element $a \in A$
$\Rightarrow a \in A \cup B$ by definition of union
$\Rightarrow a \in A \cap B$ by assumption
$\Rightarrow a \in B$ by definition of intersection
$\therefore$ Every element of A is also in B
$\Rightarrow A \subseteq B$ (1)

Take an element $b \in B$
$\Rightarrow b \in A \cup B$ by definition of union
$\Rightarrow b \in A \cap B$ by assumption
$\Rightarrow b \in A$ by definition of intersection
$\therefore$ Every element of B is also in A
$\Rightarrow B \subseteq A$ (2)
(1)&(2) $\Rightarrow A = B$
$\therefore A \cup B = A \cap B \Rightarrow A = B$ (3)

Prove the other direction

Proof that $A = B \Rightarrow A \cup B = A \cap B$
Assume $A = B$
$\Rightarrow A \cup B = A$ and $A \cap B = A$
$\Rightarrow A \cup B = A \cap B$
$\therefore A = B \Rightarrow A \cup B = A \cap B$ (4)

Combine the two to prove logical
equivalence

(3)&(4) $\Rightarrow A \cup B = A \cap B$
if and only if $A = B$

Exercise 2C

1. If $U = \{a,b,c,d,e,f,g,h\}, A = \{a,b,c\}, B = \{c,d,e\}, C = \{b,g,h\}$

   (a) Find: (i) $A \cup B$ (ii) $A \cup C$
              (iii) $A \cup B'$ (iv) $B' \cup C$

   (b) Find: (i) $A \cap B$ (ii) $B \cap C$
              (iii) $A' \cap C$ (iv) $A' \cap B' \cap C'$

   (c) Find: (i) $A \setminus B$ (ii) $A' \setminus C$
              (iii) $B' \setminus C'$ (iv) $B \cup (A' \setminus C')$

   (d) Find: (i) $A \,\Delta\, B$ (ii) $A \,\Delta\, C$
              (iii) $A' \Delta\, C'$ (iv) $(A' \Delta\, B') \Delta\, C'$

2. Draw Venn diagrams showing $A, B, C \subset U$, shading the area representing:

   (a) $A \cup B$ (b) $A \cup (C \cap B)$

   (c) $A \cap B \cap C'$ (d) $A \cap (B \Delta C)$

   (e) $A \cup (B' \Delta A')$

3. For an operation $*$ on a set A, a left-absorbing element z is defined as any element such that $z * a = z$ for all $a \in A$, and a right-absorbing element z is defined as any element such that $a * z = z$ for all $a \in A$.

For the following operations in U, identify the left- and right-absorbing elements of U, if they exist.

(a) Union

(b) Intersection

(c) Set difference

(d) Symmetric difference

4. Prove that for any sets A and B:
$$A \cup B = A \Leftrightarrow B \subseteq A$$

5. Prove that for any sets A and B:
$$A \cap B = A \Leftrightarrow A \subseteq B$$

6. Prove that for any set $A \subseteq U$:
$$A \,\Delta\, U = A'$$

7. Define the operation $*$ on the sets A and B by $A * B = A' \cup B'$. Show algebraically that:

(a) $A * A = A'$

(b) $(A * A) * (B * B) = A \cup B$

(c) $(A * B) * (A * B) = A \cap B$

8. (a) Use a Venn diagram to show that $(A \cup B)' = A' \cap B'$.

(b) Prove that $((A' \cup B) \cap (A \cup B'))' = (A \cap B)' \cap (A \cup B)$.

9. For each $n \in \mathbb{Z}^+$, a subset of $\mathbb{Z}^+$ is defined by:
$$S_n = \{ x \in \mathbb{Z}^+ \,|\, n \text{ divides } x \}$$

(a) Express in simplest terms the membership of the following sets:

(i) S_1 　　　　　　　　　(ii) S_2

(iii) $S_2 \cap S_3$ 　　　　　　(iv) $S_6 \setminus S_3$

(b) Prove that $(A \setminus B) \cup (B \setminus A) = (A \cup B) \setminus (A \cap B)$.

Summary

In this chapter we formally examined the structure and rules surrounding sets, and encountered the algebraic concept of a **binary operation**, which combines two elements of a set under a defined rule to produce a new element.

For a set A:

- B is a **subset** of A if all elements of B are also elements of A.

- $A \subseteq B$ and $B \subseteq A$ if and only if $A = B$.

- A', the **absolute complement** of A, contains all elements not in A.

An operation $\ast$ on a set A:

- $\ast$ is **closed** on A if $x \ast y \in A$ for all $x, y \in A$.

- $\ast$ is **commutative** on A if $x \ast y = y \ast x$ for all $x, y \in A$.

- $\ast$ is **associative** on A if $(x \ast y) \ast z = x \ast (y \ast z)$ for all $x, y, z \in A$.

- For an associative operation $\ast$ acting on a set S with $x, y \in S$ and for any positive integers m and n: $x^m \ast x^n = x^{m+n}$ and $(x^m)^n = x^{mn}$.

- e is the **identity element** of $\ast$ if $e \ast a = a \ast e = a$ for all $a \in A$ and is unique.

- If $\ast$ has an identity then for a given element $a \in A$, its inverse element a^{-1} is the unique element such that $a \ast a^{-1} = a^{-1} \ast a = e$.

- For an operation $\ast$ on a set S with identity e, an element $x \in S$ is said to be **self-inverse** if $x \ast x = e$.

- $\ast$ is **distributive** over another operation $\circ$ on A if $x \ast (y \circ z) = (x \ast y) \circ (x \ast z)$ for all $x, y, z \in A$.

For sets A and B:

- $A \cup B$, the **union** of A and B, contains all elements of A, B or both.

- $A \cap B$, the **intersection** of A and B, contains all elements in both A and B.

- A and B are **disjoint** whenever $A \cap B = \varnothing$.

- $A \setminus B$, the **set difference** of A with B, contains all elements in A not in B.

- $A \, \Delta \, B$, the **symmetric difference** of A and B, contains all elements in one of A and B but not both.

- Union and intersection are mutually distributive:

$$A \cup (B \cap C) = (A \cup B) \cap (A \cup C)$$
$$A \cap (B \cup C) = (A \cap B) \cup (A \cap C)$$

- De Morgan's laws state that:

$$(A \cap B)' = A' \cup B'$$
$$(A \cup B)' = A' \cap B'$$

- To prove $A = B$, prove both $A \subseteq B$ and $B \subseteq A$.

- Subsets $B_1, B_2, \ldots$ **partition** A if

$$B_i \cap B_j = \varnothing \text{ for } i \neq j \text{ (subsets are pairwise disjoint)}$$

and

$$B_1 \cup B_2 \cup \ldots = A \text{ (the collective union of the subsets equals } A)$$

1. Use a Venn diagram to show that for any two sets $A, B \subseteq U$, the three sets $A \bigtriangleup B$, $A' \cap B'$ and $A \cap B$ partition U.

2. Use Venn diagrams to show that:
   (a) $A \cup (B \cap A')' = A \cup B'$
   (b) $\left((A \cap B)' \cup B \right)' = \varnothing$

3. Set V_2 is the set of vectors with non-zero elements in two-dimensional space, and operation $*$ on V_2 is given by:

   $$\begin{pmatrix} a \\ b \end{pmatrix} * \begin{pmatrix} c \\ d \end{pmatrix} = \begin{pmatrix} ac \\ bd \end{pmatrix}$$

   (a) Show that V_2 is closed under $*$.
   (b) Find the identity element for $*$ and determine the inverse of the general element $\begin{pmatrix} a \\ b \end{pmatrix} \in V_2$.

   (c) Establish whether $*$ is associative or commutative in V_2.

4. The binary operation $a * b$ is defined by $a * b = \dfrac{ab}{a+b}$ where $a, b \in \mathbb{Z}^+$.
   (a) Prove that $*$ is associative.
   (b) Show that this binary operation does not have an identity element.

   [11 marks]

   (© IB Organization 2005)

5. Prove that symmetric difference $*$ is distributive across intersection $\cap$.

6. Let X be a set containing n elements, where n is a positive integer.
   Show that the set of all subsets of X contains 2^n elements.

7. Define the operation $\#$ on the sets A and B by $A \# B = A' \cup B'$.
   Show algebraically that
   (a) $A \# A = A'$;
   (b) $(A \# A) \# (B \# B) = A \cup B$;
   (c) $(A \# B) \# (A \# B) = A \cap B$.

   [6 marks]

   (© IB Organization 2005)

8. A binary operation is defined on $\mathbb{Q} \setminus \{0\}$ by:

$$\begin{cases} x * y = xy & \text{if } x > 0 \\ x * y = \dfrac{x}{y} & \text{if } x < 0 \end{cases}$$

(a) Determine the identity element for $*$, if one exists.

(b) Establish whether $*$ is associative, commutative and closed in $\mathbb{Q} \setminus \{0\}$.

9. For any positive integer a, define set $K_a \subset \mathbb{Q}^+$ by $K_a = \{a^n \mid n \in \mathbb{Z}\}$.

(a) Show that K_a is closed under multiplication and division, but not addition or subtraction.

(b) Prove that $n(K_a \cap K_b) > 1$ if and only if $a = b^q$ for some $q \in \mathbb{Q}^+$.

3 Ordered pairs, relations and functions

In this chapter you will learn:

- how to structure elements in ordered pairs
- about binary relations between sets
- classification of relations as transitive, reflexive and symmetrical
- about equivalence relations
- about congruence modulo *n*
- about functions
- to classify functions as injective, surjective or bijective
- about inverse functions.

You will have met the concept of relations and functions as part of the core syllabus, and should be familiar with a wide variety of functions from all parts of the core syllabus. Previously the emphasis has been on the patterns, graphs and applications of functions, but in this chapter we shall discuss the underlying structures of functions and examine them as maps between sets.

3A Ordered pairs

In Section 2C of this option we looked at ways to compare and combine sets, but we also need to pair up elements from one set with elements from another. For example, consider a restaurant menu which lists starters and main courses. We might wish to choose one item from the list of starters and one from the list of main courses to make our meal.

S: Starters	M: Main courses
Soup	Fish
Salad	Meat
	Vegetarian

Our selection might be soup followed by the vegetarian option, or salad followed by fish.

Using formal notation, we would show that the options came from the set of **ordered pairs** $S \times M$, and would list each as a bracketed pair: (soup, vegetarian) and (salad, fish).

$S \times M$ is referred to as the '**Cartesian product**' of the two sets S and M. An element of $S \times M$ consists of an ordered pair of elements, the first from S and the second from M.

We are already familiar with this notation when applied to paired values, each drawn from $\mathbb{R}$; we generally interpret them as two-dimensional coordinates (x, y) drawn from $\mathbb{R} \times \mathbb{R}$ (which is often written as $\mathbb{R}^2$).

KEY POINT 3.1

> The **Cartesian product** of two sets A and B is denoted $A \times B$.
>
> $A \times B$ is the set of all **ordered pairs** (a, b) such that $a \in A$ and $b \in B$.
>
> $A \times B = \{(a, b) \mid a \in A, b \in B\}$

Completing the menu example above, we see that $S \times M$ contains 6 elements:

$S \times M = \{$(Soup, Fish), (Soup, Meat), (Soup, Vegetarian), (Salad, Fish), (Salad, Meat), (Salad, Vegetarian)$\}$

It is clear from the way that the product is generated that for any two sets A and B:

$$n(A \times B) = n(A) \times n(B)$$

As may be supposed from the name 'ordered pair', the order in which the pair of elements appear is significant; after all, the coordinate $(2, 3)$ is different from $(3, 2)$.

KEY POINT 3.2

> Two ordered pairs (a, b) and (c, d) are equal if and only if $a = c$ and $b = d$.

Worked example 3.1

If $\mathbb{U} = \{1,2,3,4,5\}$, $A = \{1,3,5\}$ and $B = \{2,3\}$, list the elements of:

(a) $A \times B$ (b) $A' \times B'$ (c) $B \times \varnothing$

List the elements methodically. Total number of elements will be $n(A) \times n(B) = 6$	(a) $A \times B = \{(1,2),(1,3),(3,2),(3,3),(5,2),(5,3)\}$
List the elements methodically. Total number of elements will be $n(A') \times n(B') = 6$	(b) $A' = \{2,4\}, B' = \{1,4,5\}$. $A' \times B' = \{(2,1),(2,4),(2,5),(4,1),(4,4),(4,5)\}$
$n(\varnothing) = 0$ so there are no elements	(c) $B \times \varnothing = \varnothing$

Worked example 3.2

If $A = \{1,3\}$ and $B = \{1,2\}$, plot the elements of the set $A \times B$ on a cartesian plane.

List the elements methodically. Total number of elements will be
$$n(A) \times n(B) = 4$$

$A \times B = \{(1,1),(1,2),(3,1),(3,2)\}$

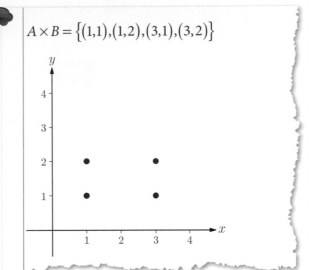

Exercise 3A

1. For $U = \{0,1,2,3,4\}$, $A = \{0,4\}$ and $B = \{2,3\}$, find:
   (a) $A \times B$
   (b) $A' \times (A' \setminus B)$

2. Plot $A \times B$ on the Cartesian plane when:
   (a) $A = \{2,3,5\}, B = \{0,1,4\}$
   (b) $A = \{1,2,4\} = B$

3. For $A = \{a,b,c,d,e\}$, $B = \{a,e,i,o,u\}$, $C = \{1,2,4,8\}$, $D = \{x^2 \mid x \in \mathbb{Z}\}$,
   find the following:
   (a) $(A \setminus B) \times (B \setminus A)$
   (b) $(A \times C) \cap (B \times D)$
   (c) $(A \cap B) \times (C \cap D)$

4. A restaurant menu has three lists of food options: Starters, Main courses and Desserts, given as sets S, M and D.

   The restaurant runs some discount 'meal deals'. The set of available meal deals is P.

   Interpret in words the following mathematical statements:
   (a) $S \cap M \neq \varnothing$
   (b) $P = (S \times (M \setminus S)) \cup ((S \cup M) \times D)$
   (c) $P \cap (S \times M \times D) = \varnothing$

5. Prove or disprove: For sets A and B, if A is an infinite set then $A \times B$ is an infinite set.

6. Prove that set union is distributive over cartesian product.

3B Binary relations and numerical congruence

Now that we have established some rules for set algebra and introduced the concept of ordered pairs, we can define the concept 'relation'. You should have encountered relations and functions already in your studies, but we can now make more rigorous definitions.

- A binary **relation** is a set of ordered pairs, and hence is a subset of a Cartesian product.

- A relation may be an arbitrary subset of a Cartesian product, but there is usually some underlying rule governing which elements appear within the relation.

As with operations, there are relations on ordered triples, and indeed any n-tuples. We shall only be investigating the properties of binary operations, and so for simplicity, subsequent references will be to 'relation' rather than 'binary relation'.

Most of the examples in this text and in the examination will focus on the algebraic and numerical, but relations, like sets, can cover any context.

For example:

1. $C = \{\text{colours}\}$, $D = \{\text{France, Japan, Sweden}\}$
   define relation R by:

   $(c,d) \in R$ if and only if c is a colour in the national flag of d

   then:

   $R = \{(\text{blue, France}), (\text{blue, Sweden,}), (\text{red, France}), (\text{red, Japan}),$

   $(\text{white, France}), (\text{white, Japan}), (\text{yellow, Sweden})\}$

2. $A = \{1,2,3,4,5\}$, $B = \{2,3,4,5\}$
   define relation R by:

   $(a,b) \in R$ if and only if $a > b$ for $a \in A$, $b \in B$

   then:

   $R = \{(3,2),(4,2),(4,3),(5,2),(5,3),(5,4)\}$

The terminology and notation for relations is as follows:

If an ordered pair $(a,b) \in R$, we can also write aRb

Since $R \subseteq A \times B$, R is said to be a relation from A to B.

Notice that in the second example, not all values of A or of B appeared within the relation set.

If we consider the subset of each of A and B for which values appear as the left and right respectively of ordered pairs in R:

$$V = \{a \in A \,|\, (a,b) \in R \text{ for some } b \in B\} = \{3,4,5\}$$

$$W = \{b \in B \,|\, (a,b) \in R \text{ for some } a \in A\} = \{2,3,4\}$$

V is called the **domain** of R and W is called the **range** of R.

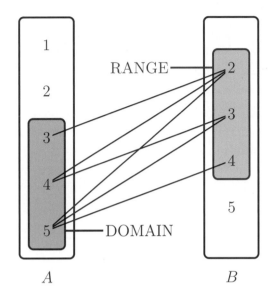

A B

In other texts, you may meet the words 'image' and 'codomain'.

The image of a binary relation (or function) is the set of values appearing as the right-side values in the ordered pairs; the definition we have used for 'range' W.

The set from which the image is drawn (B in the example) is referred to as the 'codomain', but you should be aware that in some texts, the working definitions of 'range' and 'codomain' can vary.

KEY POINT 3.3

A relation R is a set of ordered pairs: $R \subseteq A \times B$ for some sets A and B.

The **domain** of R is the set $V \subseteq A$ containing all elements of A occurring as the first component of an element of R.

The **range** of R is the set $W \subseteq B$ containing all elements of B occurring as the second component of an element of R.

Frequently we shall encounter cases where sets A and B are the same; that is, $R \subseteq A \times A$. In this case, we describe R as a relation 'in A', rather than 'from A to A'.

Worked example 3.3

Relation R is defined in $\mathbb{Z}^+$ by $R = \{(a,b) \,|\, a^3 + b^2 < 20\}$.

List all elements of R, and determine its range and domain.

List the elements methodically

$R = \{(1,1),(1,2),(1,3),(1,4),(2,1),(2,2),(2,3)\}$

Domain of R is $\{1,2\}$

Range of R is $\{1,2,3,4\}$

Worked example 3.4

$A = \{3,4,5\}, B = \{8,9,10,11,12,13\}$.

A relation R from A to B exists where aRb if and only if $|a-b|$ is a multiple of 5.

List all elements of R, and determine its range and domain.

List the elements methodically

$R = \{(3,8), (3,13),(4,9),(5,10)\}$

Domain of R is $\{3,4,5\}$
Range of R is $\{8,9,10,13\}$

We use modular addition every day when considering time. Imagine a standard (analogue) clock-face: Four o'clock plus 7 hours gives eleven o'clock ($4 + 7 = 11$). However, eleven o'clock plus 7 hours gives six o'clock ($11 + 7 = 6$). When considering hours of the day, we work in modulo 12 (or 24).

The relation in Worked example 3.4 is one to which we shall be returning frequently in the coming sections, and is referred to as **congruence modulo** (or mod) 5. An alternative way of looking at this is that any two numbers which are congruent (mod 5) will have the same remainder when divided by 5.

KEY POINT 3.4

Two values $x, y \in \mathbb{Z}$ are said to be **congruent (mod n)** if and only if the difference between x and y is a multiple of n. We write $x = y \pmod n$ to indicate that x is congruent to y (mod n).

The set of possible values (mod n) is typically denoted $\mathbb{Z}_n = \{0,1,2,\ldots,n-1\}$.

Worked example 3.5

Which of the following statements are true?

(a) $13 = 7 \pmod 3$ (b) $21 = 6 \pmod 9$ (c) $3 = 23 \pmod 5$

$x = y \pmod n \Leftrightarrow n$ divides $|x - y|$

(a) True: $13 - 7 = 6 = 2 \times 3$
(b) False: $21 - 6 = 15$, not a multiple of 9
(c) True: $3 - 23 = -20 = -4 \times 5$

> **EXAM HINT**
>
> Notice that it does not matter whether the difference is a positive or negative multiple of n.

Exercise 3B

1. State the domain and range of:
   (a) (i) $\{(0,0),(1,0),(1,1),(2,2),(3,4)\}$
       (ii) $\{(3,5),(4,1),(6,3),(8,1)\}$
   (b) (i) $\{(x,y)\in\mathbb{Z}^2 \mid x=2y+1, 0\le y<4\}$
       (ii) $\{(a,b)\in\mathbb{Z}^2 \mid a^2-2a=b, b<6\}$
   (c) (i) $R\subset\{1,2,3,4\}\times\{2,3,4,5,6\}$ where
       $$xRy \Leftrightarrow |x^2-6|<y$$
       (ii) $R\subset\{a,b,c,d,e,f\}\times\{big,bad,ugly,wolf\}$ where
       $$xRy \Leftrightarrow \text{letter } x \text{ appears in word } y$$

2. List the elements of the following relations R from A to B where $A=\{1,2,3,4\}, B=\{1,3,5,7,9,11\}$:
   (a) (i) $xRy \Leftrightarrow x=y\,(\mathrm{mod}\,4)$
       (ii) $xRy \Leftrightarrow x=y+1\,(\mathrm{mod}\,5)$
   (b) (i) $xRy \Leftrightarrow (x-y)^2=(x+y)^2\,(\mathrm{mod}\,18)$
       (ii) $xRy \Leftrightarrow x^2=y^2+1\,(\mathrm{mod}\,6)$

3C Classifying relations

Consider three relations R, S and T over $\mathbb{Z}$, given by:

$$xRy \quad \text{whenever} \quad x=y\,(\mathrm{mod}\,5)$$
$$xSy \quad \text{whenever} \quad x=1-y$$
$$xTy \quad \text{whenever} \quad x^2\le(y+1)^2$$

As in chapter 2 of this option, we can classify some common properties of relations, and we shall use these three examples.

We saw in Worked example 3.5 that if $x=y(\mathrm{mod}\,5)$ then $x-y$ must be a multiple of 5. Since 0 is a multiple of 5, it must always be true that $x=x(\mathrm{mod}\,5)$, so

$$xRx \text{ is true for all } x$$

We know that $x=1-x$ can never be true for an integer x, so

$$xSx \text{ is never true}$$

For all non-negative integers, $x^2\le(x+1)^2$, but the reverse is true for negative integers, so

$$xTx \text{ is sometimes true.}$$

Reflexive relations

A relation R in a set A is termed **reflexive** if xRx for all $x\in A$.

Note that we require that the domain of R must be the whole of set A.

In our examples, R is reflexive, but neither S nor T is reflexive.

Worked example 3.6

Which of the following relations are reflexive?

(a) Relation R in $\mathbb{Z}$ where xRy if and only if x is a divisor of y.

(b) Relation R in $\mathbb{Z}$ where xRy if and only if $x < y$.

(c) Relation R in $\mathbb{N}$ where $R = \{(1,1), (1,3)\,(3,1), (3,3), (3,4), (4,3), (4,4)\}$.

(d) Relation R in $a^2 = b^2$ where xRy if and only if $|x - y| \leq 1$.

(e) Relation R in the set of all triangles where xRy if and only if x is similar to y.

(f) Relation R in the set of all human twins where xRy if and only if x is a sibling of y.

Check that the domain of R is the whole set and that for every $x \in A$, xRx

(a) Reflexive; each value is its own divisor

(b) Not reflexive; $x \not< x$ for any $x \in \mathbb{Z}$

(c) Not reflexive; the domain of R is not the whole of $\mathbb{N}$ (however, R in $\{1, 3, 4\}$ would be a reflexive relation)

(d) Reflexive; $|x - x| = 0 \leq 1$ for all $x \in \mathbb{R}$

(e) Reflexive; every triangle is self-similar

(f) Not reflexive; although the domain of R is the whole set, no individual is sibling to him or herself

Again, consider R, S and T as given previously:

$$xRy \Leftrightarrow x = y \pmod 5$$

$$xSy \Leftrightarrow x = 1 - y$$

$$xTy \Leftrightarrow x^2 \leq (y + 1)^2$$

we notice that because R is only concerned with the difference between x and y:

$$xRy \text{ whenever } yRx$$

Similarly, we see that xSy means that $x + y = 1$, so:

$$xSy \text{ whenever } ySx$$

However, we know that:

$$xTy \text{ does not in general imply } yTx$$

Symmetric relations

A relation R in a set A is **symmetric** if, for all $x, y \in A$, xRy if and only if yRx.

In other words, any pair of elements of A are related in either direction or not at all.

Worked example 3.7

Which of the following relations are symmetric?

(a) Relation R in $\mathbb{Z}$ where xRy if and only if x is a divisor of y.

(b) Relation R in $\mathbb{Z}$ where xRy if and only if $x < y$.

(c) Relation R in $\mathbb{N}$ where R = {(1,1), (1,3), (3,1), (3,3), (3,4), (4,3), (4,4)}.

(d) Relation R in $\mathbb{R}$ where xRy if and only if $|x - y| \leq 1$.

(e) Relation R in the set of all triangles where xRy if and only if x is similar to y.

(f) Relation R in the set of all human twins where xRy if and only if x is a sibling of y.

> Either demonstrate that the symmetry property must always hold or find a counter-example

(a) Not symmetric; for example, $(1,2) \in R$ since 1 is a divisor of 2. However, $(2,1) \notin R$

(b) Not symmetric; for example, $(0,1) \in R$ since $0 < 1$. However, $(1,0) \notin R$

(c) Symmetric. For every $(x, y) \in R$, $(y, x) \in R$

(d) Symmetric: $|x - y| \leq 1 \Leftrightarrow |y - x| \leq 1$

(e) Symmetric; if triangle x is similar to y then y is similar to x

(f) Symmetric; if x is a sibling of y then y is a sibling of x

If a relation is not symmetric, it is described as non-symmetric.

If a relation in A never contains both (x, y) and (y, x) for any distinct elements $x, y \in A$, then it is described as anti-symmetric. In Worked example 3.7, (b) is anti-symmetric.

Transitive relations

A relation R in a set A is **transitive** if, for all $a, b, c \in A$, aRb and bRc implies aRc.

Worked example 3.8

Which of the following relations are transitive?

(a) Relation R in $\mathbb{Z}$ where xRy if and only if x is a divisor of y.

(b) Relation R in $\mathbb{Z}$ where xRy if and only if $x < y$.

(c) Relation $R = \{(1,3),(2,8),(3,4),(4,6)\}$ where $A = \{1,2,3,4\}$.

(d) Relation R in $\mathbb{R}$ where xRy if and only if $|x - y| \leq 1$.

(e) Relation R in the set of all triangles where xRy if and only if x is similar to y.

(f) Relation R in the set of all human twins where xRy if and only if x is a sibling of y.

continued . . .

Either demonstrate that the transitivity property must always hold or find a counter-example

(a) Transitive; if x is a divisor of y and y is a divisor of z, it follows that x is a divisor of z

(b) Transitive; if $x < y$ and $y < z$ then $x < z$

(c) Not transitive; $1R3$ and $3R4$ but it is not the case that $1R4$, since $(1, 4) \notin R$

(d) Not transitive; for example, $1R2$ and $2R3$ but it is not the case that $1R3$ since $|1 - 3| = 2 > 1$

(e) Transitive; if x is similar to y and y is similar to z, then x is similar to z

(f) Not transitive; consider twins x and y. xRy and yRx, but it is not true that xRx

Empty relations

An empty relation R is defined as a relation with no elements: $R = \varnothing$ (for example, R in $\mathbb{Q}$ where xRy whenever $x^2 = 2y^2$).

Worked example 3.9

Which of the properties of reflexivity, symmetry and transitivity apply to an empty relation R in a non-empty set A?

Apply the definitions

R is not reflexive, since that property requires that $(x, x) \in R$ for all $x \in A$, and A is non-empty.

R is symmetric, since that property requires that $(x, y) \in R$ whenever $(y, x) \in R$. Since $\varnothing$ contains no ordered pair whose reversed pair is not present, the symmetry condition is satisfied.

R is transitive; as with symmetry, the transitivity property makes a requirement based on elements present in the relation, and with no such elements, transitivity holds.

In some texts, if R is an equivalence relation, the notation $x \sim_R y$ or simply $x \sim y$ is used instead of xRy to denote 'x is equivalent to y under relation R'. We shall not use this notation.

Equivalence relations

If a relation in a set A is reflexive, symmetric and transitive, it is termed an **equivalence relation** in A.

Worked example 3.10

For any $n \in \mathbb{Z}^+$, show that congruence modulo n is an equivalence relation on $\mathbb{Z}$.

First, clearly define what is meant by congruence modulo n

Let R be the relation 'congruent modulo n'.
For $x, y \in \mathbb{Z}$, $xRy \Leftrightarrow x - y = kn$ for some $k \in \mathbb{Z}$

continued . . .

Apply the definitions to demonstrate reflexivity, symmetry and transitivity

Proof of reflexivity:
For all $x \in \mathbb{Z}$, $x - x = 0 = 0n$
$\Leftrightarrow xRx$ for all $x \in \mathbb{Z}$
$\therefore R$ is reflexive

Proof of symmetry:
Suppose xRy
$\Leftrightarrow x - y = kn$ for some $k \in \mathbb{Z}$
$\Leftrightarrow y - x = -kn$,
$\Leftrightarrow yRx$
$\therefore R$ is symmetric

Proof of transitivity:
Suppose xRy and yRz
$\Leftrightarrow x - y = k_1 n$ and $y - z = k_2 n$ for some $k \in \mathbb{Z}$
$\Rightarrow x - z = (k_1 + k_2)n$ where $k_1 + k_2 \in \mathbb{Z}$
$\Rightarrow x - z = mn$, where $m \in \mathbb{Z}$
$\Leftrightarrow xRz$
$\therefore R$ is transitive

R is an equivalence relation

Equivalence classes and partitions

We have established that congruence modulo n is always an equivalence relation. Taking $n = 3$, we can separate $\mathbb{N}$ into three subsets:

$$A_0 = \{0, 3, 6, 9, 12, \ldots\} = \{3k \mid k \in \mathbb{N}\}$$
$$A_1 = \{1, 4, 7, 10, 13, \ldots\} = \{3k + 1 \mid k \in \mathbb{N}\}$$
$$A_2 = \{2, 5, 8, 11, 14, \ldots\} = \{3k + 2 \mid k \in \mathbb{N}\}$$

Every element in A_0 is equivalent to every other element in A_0 under the relation; the same is clearly true for A_1 and A_2.

Notice that we could describe A_0 as 'the set of all elements equal to 0, modulo 3', but equally 'the set of all elements equal to 9, modulo 3', or any other element in A_0. We use the notation $\hat{x}$ ($[x]$ or $|x|$ in some texts) to indicate the set of all elements equivalent to element x.

Hence $A_0 = \hat{0} = \hat{3} = \hat{6} = \ldots$

Each of A_0, A_1 and A_2 is termed an **equivalence class** under the equivalence relation congruence modulo 3.

KEY POINT 3.5

An **equivalence class** $\hat{x}$ within a set A under an equivalence relation R is the set of all elements equivalent to $x \in A$.

$$\hat{x} = \{y \in A \mid yRx\}$$

 A relation which is reflexive, transitive and *anti-symmetric* is called an *order relation*.

Relations such as $\leq$, $\geq$ on $\mathbb{R}$ are called 'total orders' because for every distinct a, b either $a \leq b$ or $b \leq a$, whereas divisibility on $\mathbb{Z}^+$ ($aRb \Leftrightarrow b$ is an integer multiple of a) is a 'partial order', and does not have the totality property. Investigate or devise other order relations.

 We have now established the concept of an equivalence relation.

The most well known equivalence relation is '='... but we have used the equals sign many times in building the concept of equivalence relation!

Does this circularity invalidate the entire foundation of what we have developed?

The nature of an equivalence relation means that any set can be partitioned by the equivalence classes of an equivalence relation, since equivalence classes are mutually exclusive, and every element of the set lies within an equivalence class.

Worked example 3.11

Prove that the equivalence classes of an equivalence relation R in U partition U.

Define partition	Subsets $A_1, A_2, A_3, \ldots$ partition U if $A_i \cap A_j = \emptyset$ for $i \neq j$ (the sets are disjoint) and $A_1 \cup A_2 \cup A_3 \cup \ldots = U$ (every element in U is in one of the subsets)
Prove disjoint – use contradiction	Call the equivalence classes $A_1, A_2, \ldots$, Suppose A_i and A_j are not disjoint. Then there is an element $x \in A_i \cap A_j$ By definition of equivalence classes, $x \in A_i \Leftrightarrow A_i = \hat{x}$ $x \in A_j \Leftrightarrow A_j = \hat{x}$ $\therefore A_i = A_j$ Hence the equivalence classes are disjoint, since any overlap between two equivalence classes implies they are identical.
Prove exhaustive	R is an equivalence relation and therefore reflexive. $\Rightarrow xRx$ for all $x \in U$ $\Rightarrow$ For every $x \in U$ there is an equivalence class $\hat{x}$ such that $x \in \hat{x}$ $\Rightarrow$ There is no element of U which does not lie within an equivalence class $\therefore A_1 \cup A_2 \cup A_3 \cup \ldots = U$ $\therefore U$ is partitioned by the equivalence classes of R

Exercise 3C

1. State the domain and range of:
   (a) (i) $R = \{(0,1),(2,1),(3,2),(3,3)\}$
       (ii) $R = \{(1,1),(2,2),(3,2),(4,-1)\}$
   (b) (i) relation R in $\{1,2,3,4\}$ where $xRy \Leftrightarrow x < y^2$
       (ii) relation R in $\{1,2,3,4,5\}$ where $xRy \Leftrightarrow x+y+2 < (x-y)^2$
   (c) (i) relation R in $\mathbb{R}$ where $xRy \Leftrightarrow y = \cos x$
       (ii) relation R in $\mathbb{R}$ where $xRy \Leftrightarrow 2x+y = x^2$

2. For relation R defined by $xRy \Leftrightarrow x - y > 2$ list the elements of the relation for:

   (a) R in $\{2,3,4,5,6\}$

   (b) R in $\{-1,1,3,5,7\}$

3. For each of the following relations, determine whether it is reflexive, symmetric and transitive in $\{1,2,3,4\}$:

   (a) (i) $R = \{(1,2),(2,1),(2,2),(3,3),(4,4)\}$

       (ii) $R = \{(1,1),(1,3),(2,2),(3,4),(4,1)\}$

   (b) (i) R defined by $xRy \Leftrightarrow x + y = 5$

       (ii) R defined by $xRy \Leftrightarrow x \leq y$

   (c) (i) R defined by $xRy \Leftrightarrow \dfrac{2x^2}{y} \in \mathbb{Z}$

       (ii) R defined by $xRy \Leftrightarrow \dfrac{1}{x} \leq y$

4. For each of the following relations on subsets of U, determine whether it is reflexive, symmetric and transitive in U:

   (a) R defined by $ARB \Leftrightarrow A \, \Delta \, B \neq \varnothing$

   (b) R defined by $ARB \Leftrightarrow n(A) = n(B)$

   (c) R defined by $ARB \Leftrightarrow n(A \cap B) \geq n(A' \cap B')$

   (d) R defined by $ARB \Leftrightarrow A \cup B' = U$

5. Which of the following are equivalence relations?

   (a) R defined on the set of 2-dimensional polygons where $aRb \Leftrightarrow a$ is similar to b.

   (b) R defined on the set of national flags of the world where $aRb \Leftrightarrow a$ and b have at least one colour in common.

   (c) R defined on the set of residents of a country where $aRb \Leftrightarrow a$ is a parent of child of b.

   (d) R defined on the set of residents of a country where $aRb \Leftrightarrow a$ is a blood relative of b.

   (e) R defined on the set of residents of a country where $aRb \Leftrightarrow a$ has the same family name as b.

   (f) R defined on the residents of a country where $aRb \Leftrightarrow a$ has at least as many siblings as b.

6. Let $S = \{(x,y) \mid x, y \in \mathbb{R}\}$ and let $(a,b),(c,d) \in S$. Define relation Θ on S as follows:

$(a,b)\ \Theta\ (c,d) \Leftrightarrow a^2 + b^2 = c^2 + d^2$

(a) Show that Θ is an equivalence relation.

(b) Find all ordered pairs (x,y) where $(x,y)\ \Theta\ (3,4)$.

(c) Describe the partition created by Θ on the (x,y) plane.   *[7 marks]*

7. Let $a,b \in \mathbb{Z}^+$ and define $aRb \Leftrightarrow a^2 = b^2\,(\mathrm{mod}\,3)$.

(a) Show that R is an equivalence relation.

(b) Find all the equivalence classes.   *[10 marks]*

8. Two relations, M and N, are defined on $\mathbb{R}$ by:

$xMy \Leftrightarrow |x| \le |y|$

$xNy \Leftrightarrow x^2 + 6y = y^2 + 6x$

(a) Determine whether M is an equivalence relation.

(b) Prove that N is an equivalence relation.

(c) Determine the equivalence classes of N.

(d) Find the equivalence class containing only one element.   *[12 marks]*

9. Relation R in a non-empty set A is symmetric and transitive, and its domain is the entirety of A. Prove or disprove that R must therefore be an equivalence relation.   *[6 marks]*

3D Functions

You should remember from the core syllabus that a function f from set A to set B is a relation from A to B, with the restriction that for each $a \in A$ there is at most one $b \in B$ such that $(a,b) \in f$. That is to say, a function cannot ever be 'one-to-many'.

KEY POINT 3.6

> For any function f
>
> $(afb$ and $afc) \Leftrightarrow b = c$

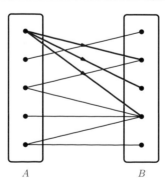

A   B

Relation: One to Many

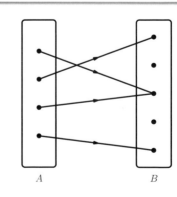

A   B

Function: Each to One

If $(a,b) \in f$ then b is uniquely defined as the only element related by f from a. We can therefore write $b = f(a)$ without ambiguity:

KEY POINT 3.7

> If f is a function from A to B then the following notations are equivalent in meaning:
> $$(a,b) \in f$$
> $$afb$$
> $$f(a) = b$$

Also, instead of the cumbersome description 'f is a function from set A to set B' we write, more briefly: $f : A \to B$.

Worked example 3.12

Determine whether relation R is a function:

(a) R is a relation in $\mathbb{Z}$: $aRb \Leftrightarrow a^2 = b^2$

(b) R is a relation in $\mathbb{R}^+$: $aRb \Leftrightarrow a^2 = b^2 - 1$

(c) R is a relation from $\{1,2,3,4\}$ to $\{5,6,7,8\}$; $R = \{(1,5),(2,7),(3,6),(4,5)\}$

> To check whether a relation is a function, determine whether the relation is ever 'one-to-many'

(a) R is not a function:
Both $(1,1)$ and $(1,-1) \in R$, so R is a one-to-many relation, not a function.

(b) R is a function:
Suppose aRb and aRc.
$\Rightarrow b^2 - 1 = c^2 - 1$
$\Rightarrow \quad b^2 = c^2$
$\Rightarrow \quad |b| = |c|$
$b, c \in \mathbb{R}^+$, so $|b| = b$ and $|c| = c$
$\therefore b = c$
$\therefore R$ is a function as it is not one-to-many.

(c) R is a many-to-one function:
$f(1) = f(4) = 5, f(2) = 7, f(3) = 6$.

Domain, codomain and range

We have already defined the relation R from A to B as a subset of $A \times B$.

We defined the domain of R as the subset $V \subseteq A$, the set of elements which appear as the left part of at least one element of R:

$V = \{a \in A \mid \text{there exists } b \in B \text{ such that } (a,b) \in R\}$

See Key point 3.3 for definitions of domain and range for relations.

We defined the range of R as the subset $W \subseteq B$, the set of elements which appear as the right part of at least one element of R:

$W = \{b \in B|$ there exists $a \in A$ such that $(a,b) \in R\}$

B is called the **codomain**, the superset containing the range.

Since a function is a type of relation, the meaning of the terms domain and range are unchanged, but it is common to further require that a function $f : A \to B$ has no unattributed elements of A. From this point on, we shall therefore use the convention that the domain of a function $f : A \to B$ is A and cannot be a proper subset of A.

KEY POINT 3.8

For a function $f : A \to B$

> The domain of f is A
>
> The codomain of f is B
>
> The range of f is $\{f(a) \mid a \in A\} \subseteq B$

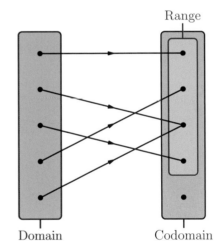

Function: Domain, Codomain and Range

For example: f is a function in $\mathbb{Z}$ such that $f(a) = |a|$ for all $a \in \mathbb{Z}$.

The domain of f is $\mathbb{Z}$.

The codomain of f is $\mathbb{Z}$.

The range of f is $\mathbb{N}$.

You may encounter a function referred to as a mapping or transformation because it directs each element in the domain to a corresponding element in the range.

f is a function from $\{a,b,c,d\}$ to $\{u,v,w,x,y,z\}$.

$f = \{(a,v),(b,y),(c,v),(d,x)\}$.

State the domain, codomain and range of f.

> Domain is the set of left values in the ordered pairs

Domain is $\{a,b,c,d\}$

> Codomain is the superset of right-hand values

Codomain is $\{u,v,w,x,y,z\}$

> Range is the set of right values in the ordered pairs

Range is $\{v,x,y\}$

Classifying functions

A function for which each element of the range corresponds to exactly one element of the domain is described as 'one-to-one' or *injective*, and referred to as an **injection**.

KEY POINT 3.9

> For an injective function f:
>
> $$f(a_1) = f(a_2) \Leftrightarrow a_1 = a_2$$

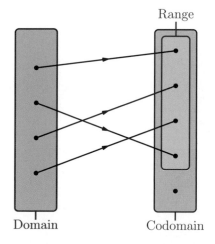

Injection:One-to-One

You may recall from the core syllabus that a function f which is continuous on a single interval domain will be injective as long as it has $f'(x) > 0$ or $f'(x) < 0$ throughout the domain; this is sufficient to prove injectivity, but notice that it is harder to determine injectivity for a non-continuous function.

$f'(x) > 0$ at all points: One-to-One

Turning curve: Many-to-One

$$f(x) = 1 - x^2 \quad f(x) = 1 + 2^{1-x}$$
$$x < 0 \qquad\qquad x \geq 0$$

$f'(x) > 0$ and $f'(x) < 0$

f is injective

$$f(x) = x + 1$$
$$x < 0$$

$$f(x) = x - 1$$
$$x \geq 0$$

$f'(x) > 0$ throughout

f is not injective

EXAM HINT

The graph of an injective function passes the 'horizontal line' test; that is, no horizontal line from the codomain crosses the graph more than once.

A function for which the range is exactly equal to the codomain is described as *surjective* and referred to as a **surjection**. A surjection f from A to B is also said to be a function onto B.

KEY POINT 3.10

> For a surjective function f from A onto B,
>
> for every $b \in B$, there exists $a \in A$ such that $f(a) = b$.

EXAM HINT

On the graph of a surjective function, every horizontal line from the codomain crosses the graph at least once.

Surjection: Range = Codomain

A function which is both surjective and injective is described as *bijective* and called a **bijection**.

KEY POINT 3.11

> For a bijective function f from A to B,
>
> for every $b \in B$, there exists a unique $a \in A$ such that $f(a) = b$.

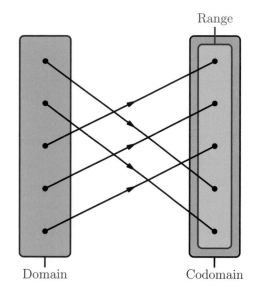

Bijection: Injection and Surjection

EXAM HINT

On the graph of a bijective function, every horizontal line from the codomain crosses the graph exactly once.

Worked example 3.14

For each of the following functions, state whether it is an injection, surjection or bijection.

(a) f is a function from $A = \{1,2,3,4\}$ to $B = \{5,6,7,8,9\}$: $f(x) = x+4$

(b) $f : \mathbb{R}^+ \to \mathbb{R}^+$, given by $f(x) = \sqrt{x}$

(c) $f : \mathbb{R} \to \mathbb{R}$, given by $f = \{(x, x^2) \mid x \in \mathbb{R}\}$

Test the properties of injection and surjection

(a) Suppose $f(a) = f(b)$
$$\Leftrightarrow a+4 = b+4$$
$$\Leftrightarrow a = b$$
$\therefore f$ is injective
There is no $a \in A$ such that $f(a) = 9 \in B$
$\therefore f$ is not surjective, and so not bijective.

(b) Suppose $f(a) = f(b)$
$$\Leftrightarrow \sqrt{a} = \sqrt{b}$$
$$\Leftrightarrow a = b$$
$\therefore f$ is injective
Each positive real value is the square root of a positive real value.
$\therefore f$ is surjective
$\therefore f$ is bijective

continued . . .

(c) Suppose $f(a) = f(b)$
$$\Leftrightarrow a^2 = b^2$$
$$\Leftrightarrow a = \pm b$$
∴ f is not injective, so not bijective
There is no $a \in \mathbb{R}$ such that $a^2 < 0$
∴ All negative real values lie outside the range of f.
∴ f is not surjective

Inverse functions

If function $f : A \rightarrow B$ is bijective, then every element of B corresponds uniquely to an element of A. We could then define a relation $g : B \rightarrow A$ as:

$$g = \{(b, a) \mid (a, b) \in f\}$$

Because f is injective, g must be a function (f is one-to-one so g cannot be one-to-many).

Because f is a function, g must be injective.

Because f has domain A, the range of g must be A, so g is surjective.

Hence g must also be a bijection.

We have:

$$f(a) = b \Leftrightarrow a = g(b)$$

g is called the **inverse function** of f, and (as is familiar) is commonly written f^{-1}.

Notice that in establishing f^{-1}, f must be a bijection; an inverse to any function other than a bijection will not be a well-defined function.

KEY POINT 3.12

For a bijective function $f : A \rightarrow B$, we define the inverse function $f^{-1} : B \rightarrow A$ by:

$$f(a) = b \Leftrightarrow f^{-1}(b) = a$$

The inverse of a bijection is itself a bijection and a non-bijective function has no well-defined inverse.

We are already familiar with an algebraic method of determining f^{-1} from f:

- for an arbitrary element x of the domain, define $y = f(x)$

- rearrange $y = f(x)$ algebraically to make x the subject

- finally restate x as $f^{-1}(y)$.

If a bijection f is given as a set of ordered pairs, f^{-1} may be
given similarly simply by reversing the order within each pair.

Worked example 3.15

For each bijective function f, give the inverse function f^{-1}.

(a) $f = \{(1,5),(2,8),(3,4),(4,6)\}$ from $A = \{1,2,3,4\}$ to $B = \{4,5,6,8\}$

(b) $f : \mathbb{R} \to \mathbb{R}$ where $f(x) = 5 - x$

(c) $f : \mathbb{R}^+ \to \mathbb{R}^+$ where $f = \{(x, x^3 + 1) \mid x \in \mathbb{R}\}$

To find the inverse of a function given as a set of ordered pairs, reverse the order of each pair	(a) $f^{-1} = \{(4,3),(5,1),(6,4),(8,2)\}$
To find the inverse of a function given by formula, let $y = f(x)$ and rearrange to find x in terms of y	(b) Let $y = f(x)$, $x = f^{-1}(y)$ $\Rightarrow y = 5 - x$ $\Rightarrow x = 5 - y$ $\Rightarrow f^{-1}(y) = 5 - y$
To find the inverse of a function given by formula, let $y = f(x)$ and rearrange to find x in terms of y	(c) Let $y = f(x), x = f^{-1}(y)$ $\Rightarrow y = x^3 + 1$ $\Rightarrow x^3 = y - 1$ $\Rightarrow x = \sqrt[3]{y-1}$ $\Rightarrow f^{-1}(y) = \sqrt[3]{y-1}$ $\Rightarrow f^{-1} = \{(y, \sqrt[3]{y-1}) \mid y \in \mathbb{R}\}$

Composition of functions

If we consider function $f : A \to B$ and $g : B \to C$, we see that by
applying f and then g, we shall ultimately map each element of A
to an element in C.

Taking the two functions together, we can describe a third,
composite function $h : A \to C$ where $h(a) = g(f(a))$ for all $a \in A$.

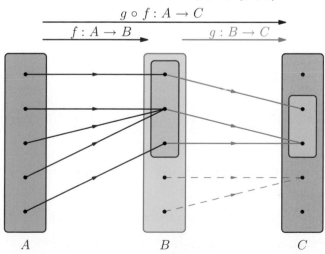

Composition of functions

In line with common practice, we shall use the notation $g \circ f$ to indicate the composite function of f followed by g, so that:

$$g \circ f(a) = g(f(a))$$

$$g \circ f = \{(a,c) \mid a \in A, b = f(a), c = g(b)\}$$

For the composite to be well-defined, we require that the range of f must be a subset of the domain of g, or there will be some element $f(a) = b \in B$ for which $g(b)$ is not defined.

KEY POINT 3.13

> For the composition of functions $g \circ f$ to be well-defined, range of $f \subseteq$ domain of g.

With what we have learned from chapter 2 of this option, we can consider composition as a binary operation on functions, and this concept will be important in chapter 4. We shall assume that the restriction imposed in Key point 3.13 is met, so that the composition is well-defined.

We first note that composition of functions will always be associative; if we consider the composition of three functions f, g and h as paths mapping each element in the initial domain to a destination in the final range, it will make no difference if we perform $g \circ f$ in a combined step and then apply h, or if we first apply f and then the combination $h \circ g$, as illustrated in the diagram below:

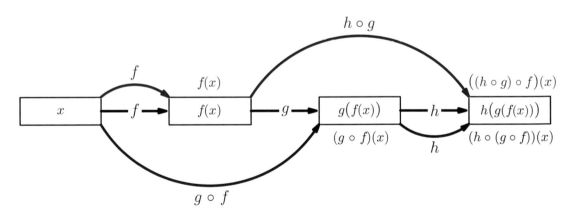

$$h \circ (g \circ f)(x) = (h \circ g) \circ f(x)$$

However, composition of functions is not generally commutative (as you should already be aware). For example:

$$f(x) = x^2 \text{ and } g(x) = x + 1$$

Then $\qquad f \circ g(x) = (x+1)^2$

whereas $\qquad g \circ f(x) = x^2 + 1$

Composition of functions is always associative, but not generally commutative.

You may see, in other texts, the identity function in a set A denoted by I_A or id_A. The International Baccalaureate® does not have a preferred notation, but we shall use I_A. If you need to use an identity function in an examination, you should define it clearly.

Continuing through our list of properties for operations, now consider the concept of an identity function and inverse functions. You are already familiar with the simple function $f(x) = x$, but now we should be a little more precise, and consider the domain associated with that function.

The identity function for a set A is a bijection $I_A : A \to A$ for which $I_A(a) = a$ for all $a \in A$:

$$I_A = \{(a,a) \mid a \in A\}$$

We can now make a further definition of inverse function, in terms of composition:

KEY POINT 3.15

For a bijection $f : A \to B$, the function $f^{-1} : B \to A$ is such that:

$$f^{-1} \circ f = I_A \text{ and } f \circ f^{-1} = I_B$$

Notice that this is a slightly more sophisticated statement than the equivalent which you may have seen previously; $f \circ f^{-1}(x) = x$, unconcerned with the difference between identity functions over different domains.

Recall that, if f and g are both bijections, then both f^{-1} and g^{-1} exist; the inverse of a composite function $f \circ g$ is the composite inverse function $g^{-1} \circ f^{-1}$.

KEY POINT 3.16

For bijective functions $f : A \to B$ and $g : B \to C$

the inverse of composite function $g \circ f$ is given as:

$$(g \circ f)^{-1} = (f^{-1}) \circ (g^{-1})$$

> **EXAM HINT**
>
> Although knowledge of the identity function is not specified on the International Baccalaureate® syllabus, examiners will expect you to understand the significance of domain to the definition of a function (as illustrated in the difference between I_A and I_B).

Worked example 3.16

Set $A = \{2, 4, 6, 8\}$, set $B = \{1, 2, 3, 4\}$ and set $C = \{6, 7, 8, 9, 10\}$

$f : A \to B$ is such that $f(x) = \dfrac{x}{2}$, $g : B \to C$ is such that $g(x) = 11 - x$, and $h = g \circ f$

(a) List the elements of h.

(b) List the elements in the range of h.

(c) Find $h(x)$.

(d) Find $h^{-1}(x)$ if it exists.

continued . . .

Remember that a function can be written as a set of ordered pairs, see Key point 3.7. Elements of the composite function $g \circ f$ are $\{a, g(f(a))\}$

(a)

$$f : A \to B$$
$$f(x) = \frac{x}{2}$$

$$g : B \to C$$
$$g(x) = 11 - x$$

$$h = g \circ f : A \to C$$
$$h(x) = 11 - \frac{x}{2}$$

$$h = \{(2,10),(4,9),(6,8),(8,7)\}$$

(b) Range $= \{7,8,9,10\}$

Compose the functions algebraically and simplify

(c) $h(x) = g(f(x))$

$$= g\left(\frac{x}{2}\right)$$

$$= 11 - \frac{x}{2}$$

A function must be a bijection to have an inverse

g is not a surjection, since no element of B maps to $6 \in C$

$\therefore$ g has no inverse

$\therefore$ $h = g \circ f$ has no inverse.

Exercise 3D

1. For each of the following functions in $\mathbb{R}$, determine the range:

   (a) (i) $f : x \mapsto x^2 + 4x - 9$　　(ii) $f : x \mapsto 3\cos 2x - 4$

   (b) (i) $f = \{(x+3, x^2 - 2) \mid x \in \mathbb{R}\}$

   　　(ii) $f = \{(x, e^{|x|}\cos x) \mid x \in \mathbb{R}\}$

2. $A = \{1,2,3,4,5\}$, $B = \{6,7,8\}$, $C = \{6,7,8,9,10\}$,
   $D = \{-3,-,2,-1,0,1\}$.

   Determine whether each of the following relations is a function, and if so, classify as injective, surjective, bijective or none of these.

   (a) (i) f from A to C: $f = \{(1,6),(2,10),(3,7),(4,7),(5,9)\}$

   　　(ii) f from A to B: $f = \{(1,6),(2,7),(3,8),(4,8),(5,7)\}$

   (b) (i) f from A to D: $f = \{(1,0),(2,-1),(2,-2),(4,0),(5,-3)\}$

   　　(ii) f from D to C: $f = \{(-3,10),(-2,9),(-1,7),(0,6),(1,8)\}$

   (c) (i) f from C to A: $f(x) = x - 5$

   　　(ii) f from D to B: $f(x) = |x+1| + 6$

   (d) (i) f from C to D: $xfy \Leftrightarrow x = y^2 + 2y + 7$

   　　(ii) f from D to C: $yfx \Leftrightarrow x = y^2 + 2y + 7$

3. For each of the following functions, sketch a graph and use it to show whether the function is injective, surjective, bijective or none of these.

   (a) $f : [1,5] \to [2,8]$, $f(x) = x + 2$

   (b) $f : [0,3] \to [1,10]$, $f(x) = x^2 + 1$

   (c) $f : [0,5] \to [1,11]$, $f(x) = x^2 - 4x + 6$

   (d) $f : [2,4] \to [1,9]$, $f(x) = 2x^2 - 16x + 17$

4. Determine whether each of the following functions is bijective and, if so, find the inverse function.

   (a) $f : \mathbb{R} \to \mathbb{R}$ given by $f(x) = 2x^3 - 1$

   (b) $f : \mathbb{Z} \setminus \{0\} \to \mathbb{Z}^+$ given by $f(x) = \dfrac{4x|x| - x + |x|}{2x}$

5. For each of the following functions, find $f \circ g$ and $g \circ f$ and so determine whether f and g commute under composition.

   (a) $f(x) = x - 3, g(x) = 2x$

   (b) $f(x) = x + 7, g(x) = 5 - x$

   (c) $f(x) = 4 - 5x, g(x) = \dfrac{2 - x}{2}$

6. For a bijection f, we define functions $h = f \circ f^{-1}$ and $g = f^{-1} \circ f$ where $\circ$ is the standard composition of functions.

   Prove or disprove: g is equal to h.

7. Define the function $f : \mathbb{R}^2 \to \mathbb{R}^2$ such that
$$f(x, y) = (2y - x, x + y).$$
(a) Show that f is injective.
(b) Show that f is surjective.
(c) Show that f has an inverse function and find it. *[12 marks]*

8. Consider the following functions:
$$f : \mathbb{R}^+ \to \mathbb{R}^+ \text{ where } f(x) = x^2 - 6x$$
$$g : \mathbb{R}^2 \to \mathbb{R}^2 \text{ where } g(x, y) = (x + y, 3x - y)$$
$$h : \mathbb{R}^+ \times \mathbb{R}^+ \to \mathbb{R}^+ \times \mathbb{R}^+ \text{ where } h(x, y) = (2x + y, xy)$$
(a) Explain why f is not surjective.
(b) Explain why g has an inverse and find g^{-1}.
(c) Determine, with reasons, whether gh is injective or surjective. *[16 marks]*

9. Let $f(x) = x^2 - 4|x - 2| - 4$.
(a) The function g is defined by
$$g :\,]-\infty, 2] \to \mathbb{R}, \text{ where } g(x) = f(x).$$
Find the range of g and determine whether it is an injection.
(b) The function h is defined by
$$h : [0, \infty[\to [-12, \infty[, \text{ where } h(x) = f(x).$$
Show that h has an inverse and find this inverse. *[15 marks]*

Summary

In this chapter we introduced the concept of ordered pairs and the Cartesian product of two sets. Then we considered relations and finally functions as subsets of Cartesian products, under specified restrictions.

- **Cartesian product** $A \times B$ is the set of **ordered pairs** $\{(a, b) \mid a \in A, b \in B\}$.

  Two ordered pairs (a, b) and (c, d) are equal if and only if $a = c$ and $b = d$.

- **Relation** R between A and B is a subset of $A \times B$, defined either as a list or according to a membership rule.

- The **domain** of a relation R is the set of left-side values in the ordered pairs of R.

- The **range** of a relation R is the set of right-side values in the ordered pairs of R.

- Two integers are **congruent modulo** n if they have the same remainder when divided by n; that is, if x and y are congruent (mod n), then $x - y$ is a multiple of n.

- A relation R on A (from A to A) is:

  - **reflexive** if xRx for all $x \in A$

  - **symmetric** if $xRy \Leftrightarrow yRx$ for all $x, y \in A$

  - **transitive** if $(xRy$ and $yRz) \Leftrightarrow xRz$ for all $x, y, z \in A$

  - an **equivalence relation** if R is reflexive, symmetric and transitive.

- The set of elements which are equivalent under an equivalence relation is called an **equivalence class**. The equivalence class containing element a may be denoted $\hat{a}$.

- Equivalence classes for relation R in A partition A.

- A function is a relation for which every element of the domain is related to exactly one element in the range.

- The graph of a function passes the 'vertical line' test.

- A function from A to B has domain A, range $C \subseteq B$ and **codomain** B.

- A function for which every element of the range is related from exactly one element in the domain is *injective* (1-to-1): $f(a_1) = f(a_2) \Leftrightarrow a_1 = a_2$. This is referred to as an **injection**.

- The graph of an injective function passes the 'horizontal line' test.

- A function whose range is equal to its codomain is *surjective* (onto): for every $b \in B$, there exists $a \in A$ such that $f(a) = b$. This is referred to as a **surjection**.

- A function which is both injective and surjective is described as *bijective* and called a **bijection**.

- For a bijective function f from A to B, for every $b \in B$, there exists a unique $a \in A$ such that $f(a) = b$.

- Two functions f and g are equivalent if they have the same domain A and $f(a) = g(a)$ for all $a \in A$.

- The identity function for a domain A is given as $I_A : a \mapsto a$ for all $a \in A$.

- The **composition** of two functions f followed by g is written as $g \circ f$:

$$g \circ f(x) = g(f(x))$$

  - For $g \circ f$ to be well defined, the range of f must be a subset of the domain of g.

  - The domain of $g \circ f$ is the domain of f, the range of $g \circ f$ is a subset of the range of g.

  - In general, functions are always associative not commutative: That is, $f \circ g$ is generally not the same as $g \circ f$.

- Only a bijective function f has an **inverse function** f^{-1}.

  - The range of f^{-1} is the domain of f.

  - The domain of f^{-1} is the range of f.

- For $f : A \to B$, $f \circ f^{-1} = I_B$ and $f^{-1} \circ f = I_A$.

- For bijective functions $f : A \to B$ and $g : B \to C$, the inverse of the composite function $g \circ f$ is given as $(g \circ f)^{-1} = (f^{-1}) \circ (g^{-1})$.

Mixed examination practice 3

1. Relation R is defined in $\mathbb{C}$ by:
$$wRz \Leftrightarrow w^3|z|^3 = z^3|w|^3$$

   (a) Show that R is an equivalence relation on $\mathbb{C}$.

   (b) Draw the locus on the Argand plane of all values in the
       equivalence class of $-i$.   *[6 marks]*

2. Relation D is defined in $\mathbb{R} \setminus \{1\}$ by
$$xDy \Leftrightarrow xy = x + y.$$

   Show that D is a function in $\mathbb{R} \setminus \{1\}$.   *[6 marks]*

3. Relation R is defined in $\mathbb{Z}^+$ by
$$xRy \Leftrightarrow x^2 = y^2 \text{ (modulo 10)}.$$

   (a) Show that R is an equivalence relation on $\mathbb{Z}^+$.

   (b) Identify the equivalence classes of R.   *[10 marks]*

4. (a) Below are the graphs of the two functions $f : \mathbb{R} \rightarrow \mathbb{R}$ and $g : \mathbb{R} \rightarrow \mathbb{R}$.

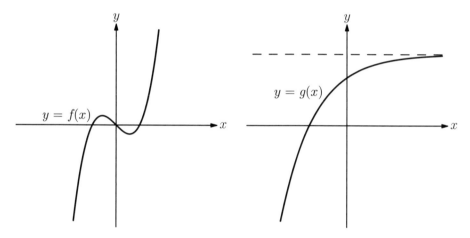

   Determine, with reference to features of the graphs, whether the functions
   are injective and/or surjective.

   Given two functions $h : X \rightarrow Y$ and $k : Y \rightarrow Z$, show that:

   (b) if both h and k are injective then so is the composite function $k \circ h$.

   (c) if both h and k are surjective then so is the composite
       function $k \circ h$.   *[13 marks]*

5. Let $S = \{2, 4, 6, 8, 10, 12, 14\}$. The relation R is defined on S such that for $a, b \in S$, $a\,R\,b$ if and only if $a^2 \equiv b^2$ (modulo 6).

(a) Show that R is an equivalence relation.

(b) Find all the equivalence classes. *[15 marks]*

(© *IB Organization 2006*)

6. Consider the set $\mathbb{Z} \times \mathbb{Z}^+$. Let R be the relation defined by the following:

for (a,b) and (c,d) in $\mathbb{Z} \times \mathbb{Z}^+$, $(a,b)\,R(c,d)$ if and only if $ad = bc$,

where ab is the product of the two numbers a and b.

(a) Prove that R is an equivalence relation on $\mathbb{Z} \times \mathbb{Z}^+$.

(b) Show how R partitions $\mathbb{Z} \times \mathbb{Z}^+$, and describe the equivalence classes. *[6 marks]*

7. Consider the following functions.

$f : \mathbb{R}^+ \to \mathbb{R}^+$ where $f(x) = x^2 + 3x + 2$

$g : \mathbb{R} \times \mathbb{R} \to \mathbb{R} \times \mathbb{R}$ where $g(x, y) = (3x + 2y, 2x + y)$

$h : \mathbb{R}^+ \times \mathbb{R}^+ \to \mathbb{R}^+ \times \mathbb{R}^+$ where $h(x, y) = (x + y, xy)$

(a) Explain why f is not surjective.

(b) Explain why g has an inverse, and find g^{-1}.

(c) Determine, with reasons, whether h is

    (i) injective;

    (ii) surjective. *[16 marks]*

(© *IB Organization 2006*)

8. Let $S = \mathbb{Z}^+ \setminus \{1\}$. The relation R is defined on S by:

$mRn \Leftrightarrow \gcd(m,n) > 1$, for $m, n \in S$.

(a) Show that R is reflexive.

(b) Show that R is symmetric.

(c) Show, using a counter example, that R is not transitive. *[11 marks]*

9. The function f is defined by:

$$f : \mathbb{R} \to \mathbb{R} \quad \text{where} \quad f(x) = 1 + e^{\cos 2x}$$

(a) Find the exact range, A, of f.

(b) Explain why f is not an injection.

(c) Giving a reason, state whether or not f is a surjection.

The function g is now defined to be $g : [-k, k] \to A$, where $g(x) = e^{\sin x} + 1$ and $k > 0$.

(d) Find the maximum value of k for which g is an injection.

For this value of k,

(e) find an expression for $g^{-1}(x)$

(f) write down the domain of g^{-1}. *[15 marks]*

10. An operation $*$ is defined on $\mathbb{Q}^+$ by:

$$x * y = \frac{\min(x, y)}{\max(x, y)}$$

The function $f : \mathbb{Q}^+ \times \mathbb{Q}^+ \to \mathbb{Q}^+$ is given by:

$$f(x, y) = x * y$$

(a) The range, R, of f is given as $R = \{q \in Q \mid a < q \leq b\}$.

Determine the values of a and b.

The function $f_K : K \to R$ is given by $f_K(x, y) = x * y$ where $K \subset \mathbb{Z}^+ \times \mathbb{Z}^+$.

(b) For $K = \{(x, y) \mid x < y, \gcd(x, y) = 1\}$, show that f_K is a bijection.

[12 marks]

4 Groups and subgroups

When we studied binary operations in chapter 2 of this option, we encountered properties such as closure and associativity which were common to many operations. In this chapter we shall concentrate on operations which share some of those important properties, even if the objects they act on are completely different. We know that an operation acts to combine two elements of a set (the operands) and form a resultant element. By linking a set with an operation in that set, and then placing certain requirements upon the operation, we form a structure which we call a group.

As with all the topics encountered in this option, group theory is abstract; indeed, this is the source of its richness. In advanced group theory, we can strip down a mathematical problem into its base algebraic structure, and by mapping this to another, more accessible structure, can produce elegant and simple results which are difficult to find in the original context.

This chapter only introduces group structure and elementary group theory, but with a couple of fundamental results and some illustrative examples, it should provide a sound basis for further study in this field of mathematics.

In this chapter you will learn:

- about the definition and structure of a group
- about cyclic groups and generator elements
- about subgroups and their orders
- about functions which map one group to another which preserve structure (homomorphisms)
- about bijective homomorphisms (isomorphisms)
- about applied groups, including groups of symmetry and permutation.

4A Group structure

Consider the binary operation of multiplication over the set $S = \{1, i, -1, -i\} \subset \mathbb{C}$.

In Section 2B of this option, we analysed the properties of the operation on this small set using a Cayley table.

×	1	i	−1	−i
1	1	i	−1	−i
i	i	−1	−i	1
−1	−1	−i	1	i
−i	−i	1	−i	−1

We notice that:

- the operation is closed over S
- the identity of the operation (1) is an element of S
- since the identity appears in each row and column, the inverse of every element of S is also in S.

Furthermore, we know that:

- standard multiplication is an associative operation.

These four qualities, taken together, are the fundamental requirements (axioms) for the structure called a **group**. We would denote the group described above as

$$\{S, \times\}$$

indicating both the set and the binary operation on it.

KEY POINT 4.1

For a non-empty set G and a binary operation $*$ on G, we say that $\{G, *\}$ is a group if the following properties hold.

Closure:	G is closed under $*$
	$g_1 * g_2 \in G$ for all $g_1, g_2 \in G$
Associativity:	$*$ is associative in G
	$g_1 * (g_2 * g_3) = (g_1 * g_2) * g_3$ for all $g_1, g_2, g_3 \in G$
Identity:	G must contain the identity element of operation $*$
	There exists $e \in G$ such that $e * g = g * e = g$ for all $g \in G$
Inverses:	For each $g \in G$ there exists $g^{-1} \in G$ such that $g * g^{-1} = g^{-1} * g = e$

In Worked example 2.5 we proved that the identity element of an operation is unique.

Notice that we do not require commutativity as one of our group axioms. A group with a commutative operation is called an **Abelian group.**

KEY POINT 4.2

An Abelian group $\{G, *\}$ has the additional property:

Commutativity:	$g_1 * g_2 = g_2 * g_1$ for all $g_1, g_2 \in G$

Since we know that multiplication is a commutative operation, we can say that $\{S, \times\}$ is an Abelian group.

Formally, G is a set, whereas $\{G, *\}$ is the group denoted by both set and operation. However, once the operation is established, it is standard to refer to the group as G, and we shall adopt this practice where it is not ambiguous.

In defining a group we are just listing a set of rules that we assert as true. More than ever, in this abstract mathematics, are we blurring the line between 'creating' mathematical reality instead of discovering it?

Can we learn anything interesting if we take axioms we might normally consider to be false?

Is this sort of artificial rule-making useful in other scientific contexts, or is an approach of scientific observation and experiment more enlightening?

EXAM HINT

It is always acceptable to assert associativity without proof for:

- standard addition or multiplication in any subset of $\mathbb{C}$
- addition or multiplication modulo n in any subset of $\mathbb{Z}$
- composition of functions

Associativity should be demonstrated for other operations unless a question explicitly states that it may be assumed.

Worked example 4.1

Show that the set $\mathbb{Z}_5 = \{0,1,2,3,4\}$ under $\oplus_5$ (addition modulo 5) forms a group. Determine whether or not the group is Abelian.

Demonstrate that each of the group axioms holds; for a small finite set, a Cayley table is a useful tool for illustration

The Cayley table for $\oplus_5$ in $\mathbb{Z}_5$:

$\oplus_5$	0	1	2	3	4
0	0	1	2	3	4
1	1	2	3	4	0
2	2	3	4	0	1
3	3	4	0	1	2
4	4	0	1	2	3

Closure: The table demonstrates that $\mathbb{Z}_5$ is closed under the operation

Associativity follows from associativity of standard addition in $\mathbb{Z}$

Identity: 0 is the identity element; as seen in the table, $a \oplus_5 0 = 0 \oplus_5 a = a$ for all $a \in \mathbb{Z}_5$

Inverses: The inverse of a is $5-a$ for $a = 1,2,3,4$, and the identity is always self-inverse

$\therefore \{\mathbb{Z}_5, \oplus_5\}$ is a group

Since addition is commutative, the group is also Abelian, as can be seen from the symmetry of the Cayley table

---

EXAM HINT

It is common practice to use the symbol $\mathbb{Z}_n$ to denote the set of equivalence classes $\{0,1,2,\ldots,n-1\}$ of integers (modulo n), and this notation may be used without further explanation in an examination paper.

Exercise 4A

1. Show that the set $\left\{1, \operatorname{cis}\left(\dfrac{2\pi}{3}\right), \operatorname{cis}\left(-\dfrac{2\pi}{3}\right)\right\}$ forms a group under multiplication.

2. For each of the following, determine whether the set, together with the operation given, forms a group. If not, identify one of the four axioms which is not valid.

   (a) $\{0,1,2,3\}$ under $*$, where $x * y = |x - y|$

   (b) $\{q^2 \mid q \in \mathbb{Q} \setminus \{0\}\}$ under multiplication

   (c) $\{0,2,4,6\}$ under addition (modulo 8)

(d) $\mathbb{R}$ under addition

(e) $\mathbb{Q}$ under multiplication

(f) $\{7n+2 \mid n \in \mathbb{Z}\}$ under $*$ where $x * y = x + y + 5$

3. $S = \{0,1,2,3,4,5\}$ and operation $*$ on S is given by
$$x * y = x + y - 4 \,(\text{modulo } 6)$$

(a) Draw out the Cayley table for S.

(b) Determine whether S forms a group under $*$.   [7 marks]

4. Let $\{G, *\}$ be a group with element $g \in G$ such that $g * g = g$.

Show that g must be the identity element of the group.   [5 marks]

5. The following functions are defined on $\mathbb{R} \setminus [0,1]$:
$$i : x \mapsto x$$
$$d : x \mapsto 1 - x$$
$$r : x \mapsto \frac{1}{x}$$

Show that, together with three other functions q, s and t, which should be determined, these form a group under composition. Draw out the Cayley table for the group.   [9 marks]

6. The set $S = \{a,b,c,d\}$ forms a group under each of two operations, $\circ$ and $*$, as shown in the following group tables.

$\circ$	a	b	c	d
a	a	b	c	d
b	b	c	d	a
c	c	d	a	b
d	d	a	b	c

$*$	a	b	c	d
a	b			
b		d		
c				c
d				

(a) Copy and complete the table for $*$.

Solve the following equations for x.

(b) $(b \circ x) * c = d$

(c) $\big(a * (x \circ b)\big) * c = b$ [8 marks]

7. A group $\{G, *\}$ contains identity e and two distinct non-identity elements x and y.

Given that $x * y = y^2 * x$, prove that x does not commute with y.   [5 marks]

4B Group properties and cyclic groups

Cancellation laws

If told to solve the equation:

$$2 \times x = 2 \times 3$$

we cancel the factor of 2 to get:

$$x = 3$$

If we were constrained to *only* use multiplication in our working, and to show all steps, we might write the following:

$$2 \times x = 2 \times 3$$
$$0.5 \times (2 \times x) = 0.5 \times (2 \times 3)$$
$$(0.5 \times 2) \times x = (0.5 \times 2) \times 3$$
$$1 \times x = 1 \times 3$$
$$x = 3$$

This seems laborious, but it is important to note that if we want to solve that very simple equation using only multiplication, we need to make two important assumptions:

- multiplication is associative; this allowed us to move the brackets
- $1 \times x = x$, irrespective of the value of x

Further, in order to start the problem at all, we needed to select 0.5 to multiply each side of the equation. Why 0.5? We know that is the only value which when multiplied by 2 will yield 1, and we need 1 in order to apply our second assumption.

In the language of operations, 1 is the identity of multiplication, and 0.5 is the inverse of 2 under multiplication.

Because a group must contain inverses for each of its elements, we can consider the idea of **cancellation**, though in a non-Abelian group care must be taken to distinguish between left-cancellation and right-cancellation.

KEY POINT 4.3

> Left-cancellation:
>
> For $a, b, c \in \{G, *\}$ $\qquad a * b = a * c \Leftrightarrow b = c$
>
> Right-cancellation:
>
> For $a, b, c \in \{G, *\}$ $\qquad b * a = c * a \Leftrightarrow b = c$

A proof of the left-cancellation principle follows the structure given in the algebraic problem above.

Take group $\{G, *\}$ with $a, b, c \in G$.

Suppose $a * b = a * c$.

$$\Leftrightarrow a^{-1} * (a * b) = a^{-1} * (a * c) \quad \text{Inverses exist in } G \text{ (group axiom)}$$
$$\Leftrightarrow (a^{-1} * a) * b = (a^{-1} * a) * c \quad \text{Associativity (group axiom)}$$
$$\Leftrightarrow \qquad\qquad e * b = e * c \qquad\qquad a^{-1} * a = e$$
$$\Leftrightarrow \qquad\qquad\quad b = c \qquad\qquad\quad \text{Property of identity}$$

EXAM HINT

Take care that you do not mix the cancellations. Except in an Abelian group, it is not generally true that $a * b = c * a \Leftrightarrow b = c$

See Exercise 4A question 5 for an example of a non-Abelian group.

Notice that in any proof regarding groups, we should quote the group property which justifies each logical step.

The cancellation prinicple can be used to establish an interesting property of a Cayley table of a group. Look again at the Cayley table from Worked example 4.1:

$\oplus_5$	0	1	2	3	4
0	0	1	2	3	4
1	1	2	3	4	0
2	2	3	4	0	1
3	3	4	0	1	2
4	4	0	1	2	3

We can see that every row contains a single instance of each member of the group, and the same is true for every column. This '**Latin square**' property of the table is common to all groups, finite or infinite, and therefore is a necessary (but not sufficient) condition when checking that a set qualifies as a group with a given operation.

Worked example 4.2

Prove that for a group $\{G, *\}$, each row of the Cayley table includes exactly one instance of each element of the group.

We first need to show that there are no repeated elements in any row. It is difficult to show this directly, so try proof by contradiction.

> Suppose that in the row of element a, there is a repeated element.
> $a * b = a * c$ for some $b, c \in G$ with $b \neq c$
> But by the left-cancellation principle,
> $$a * b = a * c \Rightarrow b = c$$
> This contradicts the initial supposition
> $\therefore$ No row contains a repeated element.

Having established no repeats, we must also show that each element *does* appear (for an infinite group we cannot simply use a counting argument)

> We must show that every element $g \in G$ appears in the row of element a in the Cayley table.

continued . . .

This means that there is an element $b \in G$ such that $ab = g$. We can guess what b is, or 'solve the equation' to get $b = a^{-1}g$. We need to explain why $b \in G$.

$a \in G \Rightarrow a^{-1} \in G$ Inverses exist in G
$a^{-1} * g \in G$ Closure

But then the cell in the row of element a and the column of element $a^{-1} * g$ will contain element

$$a * (a^{-1} * g) \; (= a * a^{-1}) * g$$
$$= a * (a^{-1} * g) \quad \text{Associativity}$$
$$= e * g \quad\quad a * a^{-1} = e$$
$$= g \quad\quad\quad \text{Identity}$$

$\therefore$ Every element $g \in G$ appears in the row of element a in the Cayley table.

An equivalent set of arguments can be used to establish that each column must contain exactly one instance of each element of the group.

Worked example 4.3

Establish whether the structures represented by the Cayley tables below form a group:

(a)

*	v	w	x	y	z
v	v	w	x	y	z
w	w	x	z	y	v
x	x	v	y	z	w
y	y	z	x	w	v
z	z	v	w	x	y

(b)

*	v	w	x	y	z
v	v	w	x	y	z
w	w	y	z	x	v
x	x	v	y	z	w
y	y	z	x	w	v
z	z	x	w	v	y

Check each of the properties of Latin square, closure, identity and inverse first as these are the easiest to find a counter-example

(a) Not a group
    v does not appear in the column for y, so the Latin square property is broken.
    This cannot be a group.

(b) Not a group
    The identity element must be v since
    $v * g = g * v = g$ for all $g \in G$.
    $w * z = v$ but $z * w \neq v$.
    Hence there is no element which is both left and right inverse to w.
    This cannot be a group, as not every element has an inverse element.

> **EXAM HINT**
>
> Check associativity only if the other three axioms hold and you have not identified the group.

In both cases of Worked example 4.3 we found a reason that the table could not represent a group, but it can be more difficult to be certain that a table does represent a group; just because we can't find a flaw, it is not safe to assert that there is none!

In Section 4E we shall look in detail at some standard small group structures, which will allow us to be more confident that a given table does represent a group.

Order

The **order of a group** $\{G, *\}$ is the number of elements in G, written $n(G)$.

A group with infinite order is called an **infinite group**.

A group with finite order is called a **finite group**.

We learned in Section 2B that for an associative operator $*$, element $a \in G$ and $m, n \in \mathbb{Z}$, we write:

$$\underbrace{a * a * \ldots * a}_{n \text{ times}} \text{ as } a^n$$

Then the following laws apply, familiar from the laws of exponents:

$$a^m * a^n = a^{m+n}$$

$$\left(a^m\right)^n = a^{mn}$$

$$\left(a^n\right)^{-1} = a^{-n} = \left(a^{-1}\right)^n$$

However, only in an Abelian (commutative) group is it necessarily true that:

$$\left(a * b\right)^n = a^n * b^n$$

because we would need to reorder the elements from:

$$\left(a * b\right)^n = \underbrace{a * b * a * b * \ldots * a * b}_{n \text{ times}}$$

to:

$$a^n * b^n = \underbrace{a * a * \ldots * a}_{n \text{ times}} * \underbrace{b * b * \ldots * b}_{n \text{ times}}$$

and reordering is not always valid in non-Abelian groups.

The **order of an element** $a \in G$ is the smallest integer $n \geq 1$ such that $a^n = e$.

If there is no such integer n then element a is said to have infinite order.

Notice that e is the only element with order 1.

Worked example 4.4

Prove that for a finite group $\{G, *\}$, every element has finite order.

Proof by contradiction is once again a useful approach.

Suppose for a group G with finite order N there is an element $a \in G$ with infinite order.

Consider elements $e, a, a^2, a^3, \ldots, a^N$

There are $N + 1$ elements in that list, and by closure all must be in G, which only contains N distinct elements.

It follows that at least two of them (call them a^i and a^j with $i > j$) must be equal.

$$a^i = a^j$$

$$\left(a^j\right)^{-1} = a^{-j} \in G \qquad \text{Inverses must exist in } G$$

$$a^i * a^{-j} = a^j * a^{-j}$$

$$\Rightarrow \qquad a^{i-j} = e$$

This means that a has finite order (no greater than $i - j$)

This contradicts our assumption; we can conclude that every element in a finite group G has finite order.

In fact, we can make a more refined observation: Since i and j were both values between 0 and n, and the order of a was no greater than $i - j$, we see that the order of an element can never be greater than the order of its group.

If you are asked to prove a property of a particular group, remember you can use any of the properties of closure, associativity, identity and inverses. These, together with any restrictions on the set of elements, should always be sufficient.

> We shall see in Section 4C that, for a finite group, the order of each element must be a factor of the order of the group.

Worked example 4.5

Show that a group $\{G, *\}$ which contains no elements of order greater than 2 must be Abelian.

Use given properties to show that $ab = ba$

For any $a, b \in G$

$$a * b \in G \qquad \text{(closure)}$$

$$\therefore a^2 = b^2 = (a * b)^2 = e \qquad \text{(property of } G)$$

$$\Rightarrow \qquad (a * b) * (a * b) = e$$

$$\Rightarrow \qquad a * b * a * b = e \qquad \text{(associativity)}$$

$$\Rightarrow \qquad a * (a * b * a * b) * b = a * (e) * b$$

$$\Rightarrow \qquad a^2 * b * a * b^2 = a * b \qquad \text{(associativity)}$$

$$\Rightarrow \qquad e * b * a * e = a * b \qquad \text{(property of } G)$$

$$\Rightarrow \qquad b * a = a * b$$

If $b * a = a * b$ for all $a, b \in G$ then G is Abelian.

Cyclic groups

So far we have constructed groups starting from a set and a binary operation, and then making sure that the requirements of closure, identity, inverses and associativity are met.

Now we shall start with an operation, its identity element and a single element of finite order, and then build a minimal group to contain it.

Suppose element a has order $n = 5$ under operation $*$.

We start with set $\{e, a\}$; clearly this is not closed, since $a^2 \neq e$ (or a would have order 2) and $a^2 \neq a$ (or a would be the identity and have order 1).

If we are to build a group then we require closure, so we have to expand the set to include a^2.

By similar argument, we must also include a^3 and a^4.

We now have a set $S = \{e, a, a^2, a^3, a^4\}$. Is this sufficient with $*$ to form a group?

Remembering that a has order 5, so $a^5 = e$, and $a^6 = e * a = a$ etc., we can draw out a Cayley table for our proposed group.

$*$	e	a	a^2	a^3	a^4
e	e	a	a^2	a^3	a^4
a	a	a^2	a^3	a^4	e
a^2	a^2	a^3	a^4	e	a
a^3	a^3	a^4	e	a	a^2
a^4	a^4	e	a	a^2	a^3

Certainly we can see that we have a set which is closed under $*$.

Since all elements are of the form a^k, associativity is fulfilled.

The table is symmetrical and a Latin square, so inverses are also satisfied; a and a^4 are an inverse pair, as are a^2 and a^3.

In fact, $\{S, *\}$ as shown in the table is an Abelian group, of order 5.

Because we have built the group by taking powers of a single element a, we call a a **generator** of the group,

We describe the group as a **cyclic group** because by taking in sequence $e, a, a^2, ...$, we can cycle through every element of the set, returning to the start with $a^5 = e$, $a^6 = a$.

KEY POINT 4.4

For a group $\{G, *\}$, if there is an element $g \in G$ such that every element of G can be expressed in the form g^k for some $k \in \mathbb{Z}$ then the group is called a cyclic group and is said to be generated by g, denoted as $G = <g>$.

Extending this, we can see that any group of order n which contains an element a of order n is a cyclic group, generated by a. Using a similar argument as in Worked example 4.4, we know that $e, a, a^2, \ldots, a^{n-1}$ must all be distinct elements, and by closure they must all be in the group. There are n elements in that list, so there can be no other elements in the group; it must therefore be cyclic and generated by a.

KEY POINT 4.5

For a finite a group $\{G, *\}$ if there is an element $g \in G$ such that the order of g is the same as the order of G then:

G is a cyclic group and $G = <g>$

Note that the generating element is not unique; indeed, in the above example, any of the elements other than e would generate the same group, since each element other than e has order 5, which is the order of the whole group. For example, if we take $b = a^2$ then:

$$b^2 = a^4$$

$$b^3 = a^6 = a$$

$$b^4 = a^8 = a^3$$

$$b^5 = a^{10} = e$$

Hence $\{e, a, a^2, a^3, a^4\} = \{e, b, b^2, b^3, b^4\}$; $\{S, *\} = <a> = <a^2>$.

Worked example 4.6

Show that the set $\mathbb{Z}_5 \setminus \{0\} = \{1, 2, 3, 4\}$ with $\otimes_5$ (multiplication modulo 5) is a cyclic group and find the order of each element.

First, show that this is indeed a group. Demonstrate that each of the group axioms holds; for a small finite set, a Cayley table is a useful tool for showing this

The Cayley table for $\otimes_5$ in $\mathbb{Z}_5 \setminus \{0\}$:

$\otimes_5$	1	2	3	4
1	1	2	3	4
2	2	4	1	3
3	3	1	4	2
4	4	3	2	1

Closure: The table demonstrates that $\mathbb{Z}_5 \setminus \{0\}$ is closed under $\otimes_5$

Associativity: follows from associativity of standard multiplication in $\mathbb{Z}$

Identity: 1 is the identity element; as seen in the table, $a \otimes_5 1 = 1 \otimes_5 a = a$ for all $a \in \mathbb{Z}_5 \setminus \{0\}$

Inverses: 2 and 3 form an inverse pair, 4 is self-inverse. $\therefore \{\mathbb{Z}_5 \setminus \{0\}, \otimes_5\}$ is a group.

continued . . .

To demonstrate that this is a cyclic group, it is sufficient to find an element with order the same as the group order, since such an element must be a generator of the group

1 has order 1, since it is the identity

4 has order 2, since it is self-inverse

$2^2 = 4$, $2^3 = 3$, $2^4 = 1$, so 2 has order 4

3 is the inverse of 2, so also has order 4

Since the group can be generated by a single element (2 or 3), it is cyclic.

The above example illustrates that not *every* element of a cyclic group is necessarily a generator of the group, although the inverse of a generator will also be a generator. In fact, we can show that for a generating element a of a finite group G, a^k will be a generator of a cyclic group G if and only if k and $n(G)$ are coprime (have greatest common divisor equal to 1); see Exercise 4B question 6.

We can immediately deduce from this that all non-identity elements of a group with prime order must be generators of that group.

Exercise 4B

1. For each of the following groups, find the order of element 1:

   (a) $\{1,2,3,4,5,6\}$ under multiplication (modulo 7)

   (b) $\{0,1,2,3,4,5\}$ under $*$ where $x * y = x + y - 2$ (modulo 6)

   (c) $\{1, i, -1, -i\}$ under $*$ where $x * y = -1 \times x \times y$

   (d) $\mathbb{Q} \setminus \{0\}$ under $\times$

   (e) $\mathbb{Z}$ under $+$

2. Which of the following sets and operations form groups? If they form a cyclic group, list all generators:

   (a) $\mathbb{N}$ under addition

   (b) $\mathbb{Q}^+$ under multiplication

   (c) $\{1,2,3,4,5\}$ under multiplication modulo 6

   (d) $\{0,1,2,3,4,5\}$ under multiplication modulo 6

   (e) $\{0,1,2,3,4,5\}$ under addition modulo 6

   (f) $\{1,2,3,4\}$ under multiplication modulo 5

   (g) $\left\{\dfrac{a}{3^b} \mid a, b \in \mathbb{Z}\right\}$ under addition

   (h) $\left\{\dfrac{a}{3^b} \mid a, b \in \mathbb{Z}\right\}$ under multiplication

   (i) $\left\{\begin{pmatrix} x \\ y \end{pmatrix} \middle| x \in \mathbb{Z}_5, y \in \mathbb{Z}_7 \right\}$ under $*$ where

   $$\begin{pmatrix} u \\ v \end{pmatrix} * \begin{pmatrix} x \\ y \end{pmatrix} = \begin{pmatrix} u + vy + x \,(\text{modulo } 5) \\ v + ux + y \,(\text{modulo } 7) \end{pmatrix}$$

3. (a) Show that $\{1,3,7,9\}$ forms a group under multiplication (modulo 10). Determine whether it is cyclic and if so, list any generators.

   (b) Show that $\{2,4,6,8\}$ forms a group under multiplication (modulo 10). Determine whether it is cyclic and if so, list any generators.

   (c) Show that $\{1,5,7,11\}$ forms a group under multiplication (modulo 12). Determine whether it is cyclic and if so, list any generators.

4. Let $S = \{0, 1, 2, 3, 4, 5\}$ with $\oplus_6$ (addition modulo 6).
   (a) Find the order of
       (i) 4   (ii) 5
   (b) Write down the inverse of 4.
   (c) Find x such that $x \oplus_6 4 = 1$.   *[7 marks]*

5. Group G contains elements a and b such that $a^3 = b^3$. Given that $x \in G$ and $x * b = a^4$, show that $x = ab^2$.   *[5 marks]*

6. Prove that in a group G, if an element $a \in G$ has order n then a^{-1} must have order n.   *[4 marks]*

7. Prove that, if a has finite order, $<a> = <a^{-1}>$ *[4 marks]*

8. A cyclic group G has order n and generating element a. Let k be a positive integer smaller than n

   (a) Prove that if k is a factor of n then a^k is not a generator of G.

   (b) Suppose that gcd $(k, n) = d > 1$. By considering $(a^k)^{n/d}$ show that a^k is not a generator of G.

   (c) Prove that if gcd $(k, n) = 1$ then a^k is a generator of G.   *[8 marks]*

4C Subgroups and cosets

We learned in chapter 2 of this option that if every element of a set A is also a member of set B, we write $A \subseteq B$ and say A is a subset of B. Similarly, if every element of a group $\{G, *\}$ is an element of group $\{H, *\}$, we say that G is a **subgroup** of H.

Care must be taken however; not every subset of H forms a subgroup, since not every subset will fulfil the group axioms of closure, identity and inverses.

Associativity is automatically inherited, since if $a * (b * c) = (a * b) * c$ for all $a, b, c \in H$ then the same is certainly true for all elements in $G \subseteq H$.

KEY POINT 4.6

> For a group $\{H, *\}$, the subset $G \subseteq H$ forms a subgroup $\{G, *\}$ as long as $e \in G$ and G fulfils the axioms of closure and inverses for a group.

Worked example 4.7

Suppose $\{G, *\}$ is a group and H is a non-empty subset of G.

Show that if $a * b^{-1} \in H$ for all $a, b \in H$ then H is a subgroup of G.

Demonstrate that each of the four group axioms holds, on the assumption that $ab^{-1} \in H$	Suppose $a * b^{-1} \in H$ for all $a, b \in H$ (1)
	
	(1) $\Rightarrow$ For $a \in H, a * a^{-1} \in H$
	    $\Rightarrow e \in H$ (Definition of a^{-1}) (2)
	$\therefore H$ contains the identity element
	(1), (2) $\Rightarrow$ For all $b \in H, e * b^{-1} \in H$
	    $\Rightarrow$ For all $b \in H, b^{-1} \in H$ (Definition of e) (3)
	$\therefore H$ contains inverses for all its elements
	(1), (3) $\Rightarrow$ For all $a, b \in H, a * \left(b^{-1}\right)^{-1} \in H$, but $\left(b^{-1}\right)^{-1} = b$
	    $\Rightarrow$ For all $a, b \in H, a * b \in H$
	$\therefore H$ is closed under $*$
	Associativity is inherited from G.
	Hence $\{H, *\}$ satisfies the four group axioms and is a group.

The terminology for subgroups is the same as for subsets; the smallest subgroup contains only the identity element: $\{\{e\}, *\}$, while the largest subgroup of a group is itself. These are called the '**trivial subgroups**', and other subgroups are called '**proper subgroups**'.

In a question, you may be asked to find a proper subgroup of a given group; with no other constraints, the easiest approach is to identify a non-identity element with order less than the order of the group, and generate a subgroup from it. For a finite group, if there is no such element then there cannot be a proper subgroup.

Worked example 4.8

Find a proper subgroup of $\{\mathbb{Z}_4, \oplus_4\}$, addition modulo 4 in $\{0, 1, 2, 3\}$.

Determine the group structure of the original group	The Cayley table for $\oplus_4$ in $\mathbb{Z}_4$:

$\oplus_4$	0	1	2	3
0	0	1	2	3
1	1	2	3	0
2	2	3	0	1
3	3	0	1	2

To find a proper subgroup, look for an element with order less than the order of the group, and use it to generate a cyclic subgroup	0 has order 1, since it is the identity 2 has order 2, since it is self-inverse 1 and 3 each have order 4 $\{\{0, 2\}, \oplus_4\}$, a cyclic group of order 2, is a proper subgroup of $\{\mathbb{Z}_4, \oplus_4\}$.

Just as associativity is inherited by a subgroup, so commutativity is always inherited:

If $\{H, *\}$ is Abelian, then:

$$a * b = b * a \text{ for all } a, b \in H$$

$$\Rightarrow a * b = b * a \text{ for all } a, b \in G \subseteq H$$

$$\Rightarrow \{G, *\} \text{ is also Abelian}$$

However, it is possible for a non-Abelian group to have an Abelian subgroup; we know for example that cyclic subgroups are always Abelian, so any cyclic subgroup must be Abelian, regardless of the nature of the parent group.

Cosets of a subgroup

Worked example 4.9

Group $H = \{\mathbb{Z}_{32}, *\}$, where $*$ is addition modulo 32.

Prove that for the subset $G_4 = \{0, 4, 8, 12, 16, 20, 24, 28\}$, the multiples of 4 in H, is a subgroup of H under addition modulo 32.

Demonstrate that each of the four group axioms holds for the subset G_4

Identity:
 The identity of H is the additive identity $0 \in G_4$

Closure:
 For any multiples of 4, their sum (modulo 32) must also be a multiple of 4

Inverses:
 The identity 0 is self-inverse.
 For each $g \in G_4 \setminus \{0\}$, $g^{-1} = 32 - g$
 Inverses are present for each element of G_4

Remember you do not need to show associativity since this is inherited from the parent group, but you should assert its validity

Associativity:
 Arithmetic addition is associative

 Hence $\{G_4, *\}$ satisfies the four group axioms and is a subgroup of H.

Consider the subgroup G_4 as defined in Worked example 4.9.

$G_4 = \{0, 4, 8, 12, 16, 20, 24, 28\} = \{4k \mid k \in \mathbb{Z}_8\}$, the multiples of 4 between 0 and 28.

We can see that this is a proper subgroup, as it is clearly not the whole of H, but it does have a regular structure, taking every fourth element within $\mathbb{Z}_{32}$.

What relation to G_4 has the set $A = \{1, 5, 9, 13, 17, 21, 25, 29\}$?

Like G_4, A has a regular structure, with any pair of elements separated by a multiple of 4. It certainly is not a subgroup of $\mathbb{Z}_{32}$ (it does not contain the identity 0, nor is it closed under $*$).

We could write A as:

$$A = \{1 + 4k \mid k \in \mathbb{Z}_8\}$$

or could relate it to the elements and operation of G_4 as:

$$A = \{1 * g \mid g \in G_4\}$$

or even:

$$A = 1 * G_4$$

Although this last notation feels rather strange, as it suggests we are adding a value to G_4 as a whole, rather than to each element within it, it is the standard notation for sets like A, which are called **cosets**.

We call A a coset of G_4. To create it, we took an element (in this case, 1) of the parent group, and applied it (with the group operation) to each element of a subgroup G_4 to form a new set.

Note that since addition is a commutative operation, it makes no difference if we write:

$$A = \{1 * g \mid g \in G_4\}$$

or:

$$A = \{g * 1 \mid g \in G_4\}$$

but for non-commutative operations, as we shall see, it makes a difference whether our extra element is applied on the right or the left of the elements of the subgroup.

KEY POINT 4.7

> For a subgroup $\{G, *\}$ of group $\{H, *\}$, and for an element $a \in H$:
>
> The set $a * G = \{a * g \mid g \in G\}$ is called the *left coset of G in H, determined by a.*
>
> The set $G * a = \{g * a \mid g \in G\}$ is called the *right coset of G in H, determined by a.*

We can see that there are in fact four cosets of G_4 in H:

$$0 * G_4 = G_4 = \{0, 4, 8, 12, 16, 20, 24, 28\}$$

$$1 * G_4 = \{1, 5, 9, 13, 17, 21, 25, 29\}$$

$$2 * G_4 = \{2, 6, 10, 14, 18, 22, 26, 30\}$$

$$3 * G_4 = \{3, 7, 11, 15, 19, 23, 27, 31\}$$

If we look at $4 * G_4$, we soon realise that it is in fact the same as $0 * G_4$, and that each possible coset of G_4 in H is equal to one of the four listed above.

We can see some properties of cosets illustrated by the example of G_4 in H, which we can prove more generally.

Firstly, we see that the four cosets of G_4 in H are disjoint. We can prove that this is always the case; we start by supposing there is an element common to two cosets, and show that for this to be the case, the two cosets must be identical:

> **Property 1**
>
> Left cosets of a subgroup G in H are disjoint.

EXAM HINT

You should make sure you can prove each of these properties.

Proof:

Suppose $a * G$ and $b * G$ are left cosets of G in H, and that element $c \in H$ lies in both.

$$c \in a * G \text{ and } c \in b * G$$

There are elements $g_1, g_2 \in G$ such that

$$c = a * g_1 \text{ and } c = b * g_2 \qquad \text{(definition of cosets)}$$

$$\Rightarrow a * g_1 = b * g_2$$

$$\Rightarrow a = b * g_2 * g_1^{-1} \qquad \text{(right cancellation)}$$

But $g_2 * g_1^{-1} \in G$ (closure of G)

$$\therefore a \in b * G \qquad \text{(definition of cosets)}$$

$$\Rightarrow \text{For any } g \in G, a * g \in b * G \qquad \text{(closure of } G)$$

$$\Rightarrow a * G \subseteq b * G$$

By a symmetrical argument, $b * G \subseteq a * G$

$$\therefore a * G = b * G$$

Thus if two cosets intersect at all, they are equal.

Hence cosets are disjoint (non-identical cosets are completely separate).

We can also observe that every element of the parent group is present in one of the cosets.

> **Property 2**
>
> Every element of H lies in one of the cosets of G in H.

Proof:

For any element $h \in H, h = h * e \qquad \text{(identity element)}$

Since $e \in G$, it follows that $h \in h * G$

$\therefore$ Any element $h \in H$ is an element of left coset $h * G$.

These two properties, taken together, immediately give us:

> **Property 3**
>
> Group H is partitioned by the left cosets of any subgroup G in H.

Remember from Section 2B that a set B is partitioned into subsets $A_1, A_2, \ldots$ if the subsets are disjoint and their total union is equal to B.

The union of $0 * G_4, 1 * G_4, 2 * G_4$ and $3 * G_4$ was H itself. While that may have seemed intuitively obvious in the example of H and G_4, we now know that it is true in every case.

Finally, we could note that each of the cosets contains the same number of elements. Since they share a common structure, this is not surprising, and we can demonstrate that this is always true.

Since one of the cosets will always be the subgroup itself, we can be more precise:

> **Property 4**
>
> Cosets of a subgroup G in H have size equal to the order of G.

Proof:

Suppose G has elements $g_1, g_2, \ldots, g_k$. Then for any element $h \in H$, $h * G = \{hg, hg_2, \ldots, hg_k\}$. All these elements are distinct: if $hg_1 = hg_2$ then we would have $g_1 = g_2$ (by the cancellation principle). Hence the coset $h * G$ contains k elements, the same number as G.

Although we can be confident in the given proof of Property 4 for a finite subgroup G, it is less concrete if G is infinite. We used the argument of a one-to-one relationship between distinct elements of the coset and distinct elements of the subgroup to establish they had the same size.

With infinite sets, a one-to-one pairing implying equal 'size' becomes problematic, famously illustrated in Hilbert's 'Grand Hotel'.

As long as an infinite set can be in some way ordered, we know that the set has the same size as $\mathbb{N}$. Thus $\mathbb{Z}^+$, $\mathbb{Z}$ and even $\mathbb{Q}$ can be shown to have the same size as $\mathbb{N}$. However, $\mathbb{R}$ cannot be ordered, and is thus in some way 'bigger'. You may wish to investigate the work of Georg Cantor, one of the pioneers of set theory, who studied this concept of different types of infinite or 'transfinite' numbers.

Exercise 4C

1. Group $H = \{\mathbb{Z}_6, *\}$ where $*$ is addition modulo 6. Find all subsets of H which form subgroups under $*$.

2. F is the set of linear functions:
$$\{f : x \mapsto ax + b \mid a, b \in \mathbb{R}, a \neq 0\}$$
   (a) Show that F forms a group under composition of functions.
   (b) Show that $G = \{g : x \mapsto ax \mid a \in \mathbb{R} \setminus \{0\}\}$ forms a subgroup of F.

3. Show that $\{\mathbb{R}, +\}$ is a subgroup of $\{\mathbb{C}, +\}$ and describe the appearance on the Argand plane of a coset of $\{\mathbb{R}, +\}$ in $\{\mathbb{C}, +\}$, giving an example of a coset.

4. Group $Q = \{\mathbb{Q}\backslash\{0\}, \times\}$, the group of non-zero rationals under multiplication.

   (a) Determine which of the following sets forms a subgroup of Q:

       (i) $\mathbb{Q}^+$ (ii) $\mathbb{Z}\backslash\{0\}$

       (iii) $\{2^m \,|\, m \in \mathbb{Z}\}$ (iv) $\mathbb{Q}\backslash\{2^m \,|\, m \in \mathbb{Z}\}$

   (b) For each of the sets in (a) which do form subgroups of Q, write down the coset with $\left\{-\dfrac{1}{3}\right\}$ in Q.

5. Find a proper subgroup of $\{\mathbb{R}\backslash\{0\}, \times\}$ with two elements.

6. $G_8 = \{0, 8, 16, 24\}$ is a subgroup of $\{\mathbb{Z}_{32}, *\}$, where $*$ is addition modulo 32.

   List the elements of cosets:

   (a) $3 * G_8$

   (b) $G_8 * 13$

   (c) $24 * G_8$

7. Consider the group $G = \{1, 3, 5, 7\}$ under multiplication modulo 8.

   (a) Show that $H = \{1, 3\}$ is a proper subgroup of G.

   (b) Find the coset $5 \otimes_8 H$.   *[5 marks]*

8. $\mathbb{R}^3$ is the set of 3-dimensional vectors.

   (a) Show that $\mathbb{R}^3$ forms a group under standard vector addition.

   (b) Prove that $G = \left\{ \begin{pmatrix} x \\ y \\ z \end{pmatrix} \in \mathbb{R}^3 \,|\, x + y = 2z \right\}$ forms a subgroup of $\mathbb{R}^3$.

   (c) Give a geometric interpretation of G and of the cosets of G in $\mathbb{R}^3$.   *[8 marks]*

9. For a group $\{H, *\}$ with subgroup $\{G, *\}$, show that coset $h * G = G$ if and only if $h \in G$.   *[6 marks]*

10. Prove that any subgroup of a cyclic group must also be cyclic.   *[6 marks]*

11. For an Abelian Group $\{G, *\}$, let H be the subset of G
$$H = \{a \in G \,|\, a^2 = e\}$$

   (a) If $a, b, \in H$ show that $(ab)^2 = e$.

   (b) Hence, show that H is a subgroup of G.   *[6 marks]*

12. Consider a group $\{G, *\}$. Let H be the subset of G such that
$$H = \{x \in G \mid x * a = a * x \text{ for all } a \in G\}$$
Show that $\{H, *\}$ is a subgroup of $\{G, *\}$. [6 marks]

13. (a) Show that $G = \{1, 2, 3, 4, 5, 6\}$ forms a group under $*$, where
$x * y = x \times y$ (modulo 7).

(b) Find a subgroup H of G where $n(H) = 2$.

(c) List the cosets of H in G. [8 marks]

14. (a) Show that $K = \left\{ 1, \dfrac{1 + i\sqrt{3}}{2}, \dfrac{1 - i\sqrt{3}}{2} \right\}$ forms a subgroup of
$\mathbb{R} \backslash \{0\}$ under multiplication.

(b) List the elements of the coset $2 \times K$. [8 marks]

15. (a) Show that if $\{H, *\}$ is a group and $x, y \in H$ then
$(x * y)^{-1} = y^{-1} * x^{-1}$.

For a subgroup $\{G, *\}$ of group $\{H, *\}$, there are n distinct
left cosets. Elements $a_1, a_2, a_3, \ldots, a_n$ are drawn, each from a
different left coset of G in H.

(b) Show that $\{a_1^{-1}, a_2^{-2}, a_3^{-3}, \ldots, a_n^{-1}\}$ is a set of elements, each
from a different right coset of G in H. [10 marks]

16. The elements of a group $\{G, *\}$ are $\{e, a, b, b^2, a * b, b * a\}$, where
$a^2 = b^3 = e$.

(a) Prove that $(a * b)^{-1} = b^2 * a$.

(b) Draw the Cayley table for G.

(c) Show that $\{e, a\}$ is a subgroup of G.

(d) List the elements of the left coset $(b * a) * \{e, a\}$.

(e) List the elements of the right coset $\{e, a\} * b^2$. [12 marks]

4D Lagrange's theorem

We have already seen in Section 4B that any element of a finite
group must have order no greater than that of the group itself.

We can refine this idea considerably in the following theorem,
named after the Italian-born mathematician Joseph Lagrange
(1736–1813).

KEY POINT 4.8

Lagrange's theorem

For any subgroup G of a finite group H, $n(G)$ is a divisor
of $n(H)$.

The proof follows immediately from the properties of cosets
given in the previous section.

For a subgroup G of a finite group H:

the size of each coset must be equal to $n(G)$ (Property 4)

the disjoint cosets partition H (Property 3)

It follows that $n(H) = k \times n(G)$ where $k \in \mathbb{Z}^+$ is the number of distinct cosets.

$\therefore n(G)$ is a divisor of $n(H)$.

We can immediately deduce a number of consequences (formally called corollaries) from the theorem.

KEY POINT 4.9

> Corollary 1:   For any finite group H, the order of any element $h \in H$ must be a divisor of $n(H)$.

Proof: For any $h \in H$,

$<h>$ must be a subgroup of H (closure property of groups)

$\Rightarrow n<h>$ is a divisor of $n(H)$ (Lagrange's theorem)

$n<h> =$ order of h (property of cyclic generator)

$\therefore$ order of $h \in H$ is a divisor of $n(H)$.

KEY POINT 4.10

> Corollary 2:   For any finite group H where $n(H)$ is a prime p, H can have no proper subgroups.

Proof:

For any subgroup $G \subseteq H$,

$n(G)$ divides $n(H) = p$ (Lagrange's theorem)

$\Rightarrow n(G) = 1$ or p (property of primes)

$\therefore G = \{e\}$ or $G = H$, the trivial subgroups of H

$\Rightarrow H$ has no proper subgroups.

KEY POINT 4.11

> Corollary 3:   For any finite group H where $n(H)$ is a prime p, H is a cyclic group and every non-identity element of H is a generator of H.

Proof:

For any $h \in H$,

$<h>$ must be a subgroup of H (closure property of groups)

H has no proper subgroups   (Corollary 2)

$\therefore <h> = \{e\}$ or $<h> = H$

$\Rightarrow h = e$ or $<h> = H$

$\Rightarrow h$ is either the identity or a generator of H and H is cyclic.

Note that the converse of Lagrange's theorem does not hold in general; if $n(H)$ has a divisor d it is not necessarily true that H has a subgroup of order d, unless H is a cyclic group.

EXAM HINT

Proofs of these corollaries are examinable; make sure you can prove them if required. If a question does not explicitly require you to prove a corollary, you can simply quote any of these three results in an answer as part of your reasoning.

Worked example 4.10

Group $\{G, *\}$ has order 14, and H is a non-trivial subgroup of G. Show that for any non-identity element $h \in H$, either $h^2 = e$ or $h^7 = e$.

We need to show that the order of h is either 2 or 7. The order of an element is related to the order of the group by Lagrange's theorem	By Lagrange's theorem, the order of H must be a factor of 14.
	Since H is a non-trivial subgroup, $n(H) = 2$ or 7.
	By a corollary to Lagrange's theorem, the order of any group element is a factor of the group order.
	$\therefore$ If $n(H) = 2$ then $h^2 = e$ for $h \in H$
	If $n(H) = 7$ then $h^7 = e$ for any $h \in H$

Exercise 4D

1. Group D_3 is given by the following Cayley table:

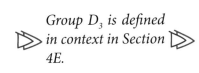

Group D_3 is defined in context in Section 4E.

$*$	e	r	s	x	y	z
e	e	r	s	x	y	z
r	r	s	e	z	x	y
s	s	e	r	y	z	x
x	x	y	z	e	r	s
y	y	z	x	s	e	r
z	z	x	y	r	s	e

Find all subgroups of D_3 of orders 1, 2, 3, 4, 5 and 6, or demonstrate that none can exist.

2. Use Lagrange's theorem to state all possible orders of:

   (a) subgroups of a group of order 18

   (b) proper subgroups of a group of order 24.

3. G is a finite group of order pq, where p and q are prime. What are the possible orders of subgroups of G?

4. Operation $\ast$ is defined on $\mathbb{N}$ by $x \ast y = x + y$ (modulo 12).

Find a subset $G \subset \mathbb{N}$ with $3 < n(G) < 12$ such that $\{G, \ast\}$ forms a group and determine whether G has a subgroup of order 3. **[6 marks]**

5. (a) Explain why the table below is a Latin square:

	d	e	c	b	a
d	c	d	e	b	a
e	d	e	b	a	c
c	a	b	d	c	e
b	b	a	c	e	d
a	e	c	a	d	b

(b) Using Lagrange's theorem or otherwise, show that the table is not a group table. **[6 marks]**

6. The set $G = \{1, 3, 5, 7\}$ forms a group under $\otimes_8$, multiplication (modulo 8).

(a) Draw out the Cayley table for this group.

(b) Use Lagrange's theorem to show that the set $H = G \cup \{2, 4, 6\}$ cannot form a group under $\otimes_8$. **[9 marks]**

7. $\{G, \ast\}$ is a group of order 15 with identity element e.

There is an element $a \in G$ such that $a^3 \neq e$ and $a^5 \neq e$.

Use Lagrange's theorem to prove that $\{G, \ast\}$ is a cyclic group with generator a. **[6 marks]**

8. Finite group G contains distinct elements a and b and identity e, such that:

$a \ast b = a^3 \ast b^4$

$a^4 \ast b^3 = e$

(a) Show that $a^2 = e$

(b) Show that the order of G is a multiple of 6. **[8 marks]**

4E Frequently encountered groups

It is useful to be familiar with common examples of lower order group structures, particularly when explaining why two groups are isomorphic.

> ▷ Isomorphisms will be introduced in ▷ Section 4G.

Groups of order 1

The only possible structure for a group of order 1 is $\{e\}$, and this is, as previously mentioned, a trivial subgroup of every group.

Groups of order 2, 3, 5 and 7

As is true for every group with prime order (see Key point 4.11), these are cyclic groups. Each has structure $\{e, a, a^2, \ldots, a^{p-1}\}$, and every element of the group is a generator, by a corollary to Lagrange's theorem.

Groups of order 4

Consider the possible orders for the elements e (identity), a, b and c:

e must have order 1, and is the only element which can do so.

By a corollary to Lagrange's theorem, every element in the group must have an order which divides the group order. If element a has order 4, then the group must be cyclic, and will have the following structure, with b and c being equal to a^2 and a^3....

$*$	e	a	b	c
e	e	a	b	c
a	a	b	c	e
b	b	c	e	a
c	c	e	a	b

$=$

$*$	e	a	a^2	a^3
e	e	a	a^2	a^3
a	a	a^2	a^3	e
a^2	a	a^3	e	a
a^3	a^3	e	a	a^2

If there is no element of order 4, then since every order must be a factor of 4, all non-identity elements must have order 2. We can construct a possible Cayley table on this basis.

$*$	e	a	b	c
e	e	a	b	c
a	a	e		
b	b		e	
c	c			e

We can fill in the details as above on the basis that e is the identity, and each of the three other elements are to have order 2, so that $a^2 = b^2 = c^2 = e$. Before we do so, however, we can note that c must be equal to $a * b$ (also equal to $b * a$) for the group to be closed.

$*$	e	a	b	$a*b$
e	e	a	b	$a*b$
a	a	e		
b	b		e	
$a*b$	$a*b$			e

Recall from Worked example 4.5 that if a group only has elements of order 1 or 2 it must be Abelian.

The remainder of the table can then be completed by direct calculation for each cell, or by observing the need for the table to be a Latin square. As the table has symmetry through the lead diagonal it is also Abelian, as we know must be the case for any group whose elements are all order 1 or 2.

∗	e	a	b	a∗b
e	e	a	b	a∗b
a	a	e	a∗b	b
b	b	a∗b	e	a
a∗b	a∗b	b	a	e

This group structure, clearly distinct from that of the cyclic group of order 4 by the order of its elements, is called the **Klein four-group**.

These are the only two possible structures for groups of order 4, and hence any group of order 4 must have structure equivalent to one or the other, determined by analysis of the order of each of the elements.

Groups of order 6

Using similar methods, we can show that there are only two possible group structures of order 6: The cyclic group C_6, consisting of $\{e, a, a^2, a^3, a^4, a^5\}$, and the smallest non-Abelian group, referred to as D_3, with group table:

∗	e	a	a^2	b	b∗a	a∗b
e	e	a	a^2	b	b∗a	a∗b
a	a	a^2	e	a∗b	b	b∗a
a^2	a^2	e	a	b∗a	a∗b	b
b	b	b∗a	a∗b	e	a	a^2
b∗a	b∗a	a∗b	b	a^2	e	a
a∗b	a∗b	b	b∗a	a	a^2	e

In the above table for D_3, a and a^2 have order 3, and b, $b∗a$ and $a∗b$ have order 2.

Groups in context

So far we have mostly considered numerical groups, with arithmetic or modular arithmetic operations; however, group theory is extremely versatile, and used in a wide range of contexts. We shall now look at two specific contexts – geometric transformations and permutations.

Geometrical transformations

Imagine a plane equilateral triangle ABC, whose upper face is shaded red and whose reverse face is shaded blue. We define a **symmetry** on ABC as any transformation which maps the triangle such that each of its three edges overlies one of the initial edge positions.

For clarity we will use the terms rotational and reflective symmetries, but we shall interpret a reflective symmetry through a line in the plane as a 180° rotation flipping the triangle over about the symmetry line.

EXAM HINT

Although you do not have to be able to prove that there can only be two group structures of order 4 or 6, we recommend that you work through the supplementary sheet 'Groups of order 6' at the back of this book on pages 125–6.

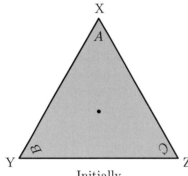

You can see that there are rotational symmetries whereby the triangle is rotated about its centre O by 120°, 240° or 0° / 360°.

There are also reflective symmetries; if we label the vertex positions X, Y and Z then (OX), (OY) and (OZ) are all lines of reflective symmetry.

We can then determine the set of all symmetries $\{e, r, s, x, y, z\}$:

e: rotation by 0° (or, equivalently, 360°)

r: rotation by 120°

s: rotation by 240°

x: reflection through (OX)

y: reflection through (OY)

z: reflection through (OZ)

If we then introduce a binary operator $*$, the composition of transformations, we can quickly see that the six symmetries form a group under $*$. Care must be taken in interpreting the order of transformations; as with functions, transformations are resolved from right to left, so $r * x$ means x followed by r.

Consider, for example, rotation r followed by reflection z, written as $z * r$:

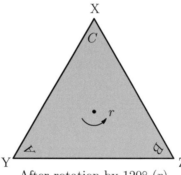

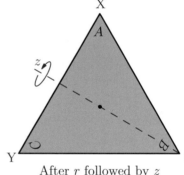

| Initially | After rotation by 120° (r) | After r followed by z |

The end position is exactly the same as would result from a single reflection about OX. We can conclude that $z * r = x$.

Notice that by considering the reverse side of the figure as being a different colour, it is clear that an odd number of reflections will always leave the shape blue side up, and an even number will leave it red side up. It is then evident that an even number of reflections will always be equivalent to a rotation, while any odd number of reflections together with any rotations must be equivalent to one single reflection.

$*$	e	r	s	x	y	z
e	e	r	s	x	y	z
r	r	s	e	z	x	y
s	s	e	r	y	z	x
x	x	y	z	e	r	s
y	y	z	x	s	e	r
z	z	x	y	r	s	e

Checking the four axioms:

Closure: Every symmetry composed with another symmetry gives a member of the set, as can be seen from the Cayley table above

Identity: Clearly the element e, rotation by $0°$, is the identity transformation.

Inverses: As seen in the table, each element has an inverse; the reflections are self-inverse and the two rotations ($120°$ and $240°$) form an inverse pair.

Associativity: If we consider the set of vertex locations $\{X, Y, Z\}$, we can interpret each of the symmetries as a bijection from $\{X, Y, Z\}$ to $\{X, Y, Z\}$, mapping each vertex from its start position to its destination. We can then argue that, as with any set of bijections, the symmetries must be associative under composition.

Hence the symmetries of an equilateral triangle under composition form a group of order 6.

Analysis of order structure shows that it is not a cyclic group; as seen on the Supplementary sheet, 'Groups of order 6': there is only one non-cyclic group structure of order 6.

We use the notation D_n, called the **dihedral group of order n**, for the group consisting of all symmetries of a regular planar n-gon. The above group is therefore called D_3.

Worked example 4.11

Determine the group of symmetries of a non-square rectangle $ABCD$ and classify the group structure.

Sketch a figure, define its symmetries and their orders. By analysis of the order of the elements, determine which of the known groups has that structure

Let a reflection through the x-axis be given as x, reflection through the y-axis be given as y, rotation $180°$ about the origin be given as r. If e is the identity transformation, then the set of symmetries is $\{e, r, x, y\}$.

Clearly, each of the elements r, x and y is self-inverse.

$\Rightarrow$ this is a group of order 4, all of whose non-identity elements have order 2.

$\Rightarrow$ this is a Klein four-group.

Permutations

Although we represented D_3 geometrically as the symmetries of a triangle, we could equally well have considered the problem in terms of the 6 possible permutations of the letters X, Y and Z.

Consider a notation where the result of each transformation is given by indicating the destination of each of the vertices with initial positions X, Y and Z.

$$e:(X \to X, Y \to Y, Z \to Z) \qquad r = (X \to Y, Y \to Z, Z \to X) \qquad x = (X \to X, Y \to Z, Z \to Y)$$

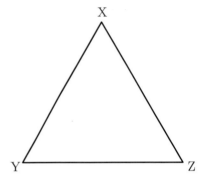

Permutation e

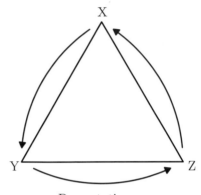

Permutation r

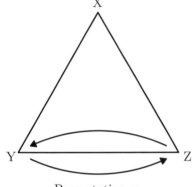

Permutation x

Each permutation is, in effect, a bijection on the set $\{X, Y, Z\}$.

In the notation of relations, we could have given r as the set of ordered pairs $\{(X,Y),(Y,Z),(Z,X)\}$, showing that

$$r(X) = Y$$
$$r(Y) = Z$$
$$r(Z) = X$$

This is clear, but writing it this way soon becomes unwieldy for permutations of large sets. A preferred option is to give each ordered pair as a column, and to write the entire bijection as an array:

$$r = \begin{pmatrix} X & Y & Z \\ Y & Z & X \end{pmatrix}$$

Similarly, we see:

$$e = \begin{pmatrix} X & Y & Z \\ X & Y & Z \end{pmatrix} \text{ and } x = \begin{pmatrix} X & Y & Z \\ X & Z & Y \end{pmatrix}$$

We shall only look at permutations on finite sets, but the following principles apply equally well to infinite sets.

A permutation on set A is a bijection $A \to A$.

A permutation $p : A \to A$ given by the set of ordered pairs $p = \{(a_1, b_1), (a_2, b_2), \ldots, (a_n, b_n)\}$, where $A = \{a_1, a_2, \ldots, a_n\} = \{b_1, b_2, \ldots, b_n\}$, is usually shown as:

$$p = \begin{pmatrix} a_1 & a_2 & \ldots & a_n \\ b_1 & b_2 & \ldots & b_n \end{pmatrix}$$

It is conventional and generally most useful if a permutation is given with the top row ordered. For example, the permutation q on $\{1, 2, 3, 4\}$ given by:

$$q = \begin{pmatrix} 1 & 3 & 4 & 2 \\ 2 & 1 & 3 & 4 \end{pmatrix}$$

would more properly be written:

$$q = \begin{pmatrix} 1 & 2 & 3 & 4 \\ 2 & 4 & 1 & 3 \end{pmatrix}$$

Each form gives the same information, since each shows the same ordered pairs which define the bijection, but the second is frequently easier to use.

Combining permutations

We can combine permutations just as we would compose any bijections, always remembering that the order of permutations within a composition is (as for any function) resolved from right to left. Thus $p_1 * p_2$, which we shall normally write more simply as $p_1 p_2$, means permutation p_2 followed by p_1.

To simplify a composition of permutations, track the destination of each element as it passes through the multiple steps. Since composition of functions is always associative, we may have several permutations in a sequence, and can resolve all at once.

Permutation applied to the roots of polynomial equations lies at the heart of Galois Theory. Using Galois Theory, we can show that roots to integer coefficient polynomials of order 2, 3 and 4 can always be expressed using only integers and radicals (square roots, cube roots etc.). We can also show that there are order 5 polynomials whose roots *cannot* be expressed in this way.

Worked example 4.12

p_1, p_2 and p_3 are permutations on set $\{1, 2, 3, 4\}$:

$$p_1 = \begin{pmatrix} 1 & 2 & 3 & 4 \\ 2 & 1 & 3 & 4 \end{pmatrix} \qquad p_2 = \begin{pmatrix} 1 & 2 & 3 & 4 \\ 4 & 1 & 3 & 2 \end{pmatrix} \qquad p_3 = \begin{pmatrix} 1 & 2 & 3 & 4 \\ 3 & 4 & 1 & 2 \end{pmatrix}$$

Express $p_3 p_2 p_1$ as a single permutation.

| Write the permutations out in order | $p_3 p_2 p_1 = \begin{pmatrix} 1 & 2 & 3 & 4 \\ 3 & 4 & 1 & 2 \end{pmatrix}\begin{pmatrix} 1 & 2 & 3 & 4 \\ 4 & 1 & 3 & 2 \end{pmatrix}\begin{pmatrix} 1 & 2 & 3 & 4 \\ 2 & 1 & 3 & 4 \end{pmatrix}$ |

continued . . .

To resolve, track each element in turn

We see that that under p_1, 1 moves to 2, which moves under p_2 back to 1, which moves under p_3 to 3

$$\begin{pmatrix} 1 & 2 & 3 & 4 \\ 3 & 4 & 1 & 2 \end{pmatrix} \begin{pmatrix} 1 & 2 & 3 & 4 \\ 4 & 1 & 3 & 2 \end{pmatrix} \begin{pmatrix} 1 & 2 & 3 & 4 \\ 2 & 1 & 3 & 4 \end{pmatrix}$$

$$3 \overset{p_3}{\leftarrow} 1 \overset{p_2}{\leftarrow} 2 \overset{p_1}{\leftarrow} 1$$

So $3 \overset{p_3 p_2 p_1}{\leftarrow} 1$

Similarly $2 \overset{p_3 p_2 p_1}{\leftarrow} 2$

$1 \overset{p_3 p_2 p_1}{\leftarrow} 3$

$4 \overset{p_3 p_2 p_1}{\leftarrow} 4$

Having determined the fate of every element, write the permutation out in standard format

$$p_3 p_2 p_1 = \begin{pmatrix} 1 & 2 & 3 & 4 \\ 3 & 2 & 1 & 4 \end{pmatrix}$$

Identity and inverse permutations

It should be clear that the identity permutation is the identity bijection. For our example set $\{1,2,3,4\}$, the identity permutation is:

$$e = \begin{pmatrix} 1 & 2 & 3 & 4 \\ 1 & 2 & 3 & 4 \end{pmatrix}$$

Also, we can see that to find an inverse to a permutation p, we can simply swap the lower and upper lines of p, (reversing the direction of the mapping) and then sort the columns by the upper element.

Worked example 4.13

Permutation p on set $\{1,2,3,4,5\}$ is given by $p = \begin{pmatrix} 1 & 2 & 3 & 4 & 5 \\ 4 & 3 & 2 & 5 & 1 \end{pmatrix}$. Find p^{-1}.

Swap lower and upper rows of p, then reorder

$$p^{-1} = \begin{pmatrix} 4 & 3 & 2 & 5 & 1 \\ 1 & 2 & 3 & 4 & 5 \end{pmatrix}$$

Sorting to standard order:

$$p^{-1} = \begin{pmatrix} 1 & 2 & 3 & 4 & 5 \\ 5 & 3 & 2 & 1 & 4 \end{pmatrix}$$

Decomposition of permutations

Consider again the three permutations given in Worked example 4.12. Rather than list all elements of the set undergoing permutation, we could restrict ourselves to giving only those which actually change, expressing the changes as cycles.

For example:

$$p_1 = \begin{pmatrix} 1 & 2 & 3 & 4 \\ 2 & 1 & 3 & 4 \end{pmatrix}$$

We see that elements 3 and 4 do not actually undergo any change, while 1 and 2 exchange places. This is described as a 2-cycle or **transposition** of elements 1 and 2, and can alternatively be written:

$$p_1 = (12)(3)(4) = (12)$$

which we read as the cycle: $1 \to 2$, $2 \to 1$, with all other elements remaining unchanged. The 1-cycles need not be written, but you should always make sure you have checked the fate of every element in the permutation set.

This is clearly a self-inverting permutation, with order 2; performing the same swap twice would take us back to where we started.

p_2 affects three elements:

$$p_2 = \begin{pmatrix} 1 & 2 & 3 & 4 \\ 4 & 1 & 3 & 2 \end{pmatrix}$$

We see that there is a cycle: $1 \to 4$, $4 \to 2$ and $2 \to 1$. Element 3 is unaffected.

We can write this as a cycle of length 3, where each element is transformed to the one to its right, and the end element is transformed to the first:

$$p_2 = (142)$$

This is not self-inverting; $(p_2)^2 = \begin{pmatrix} 1 & 2 & 3 & 4 \\ 2 & 4 & 3 & 1 \end{pmatrix} = (124)$.

However, $(p_2)^3 = e$, so p_3 has order 3.

KEY POINT 4.13

> The order of a permutation which can be expressed as a single n-cycle is n.

Finally, p_3 affects all four elements, but as a pair of 2-cycles:

$$p_3 = \begin{pmatrix} 1 & 2 & 3 & 4 \\ 3 & 4 & 1 & 2 \end{pmatrix}$$

We could write this as:

$$p_3 = (13)(24)$$

Note that this is different from the 4-cycle (1324); in p_3, we swap the first and third elements, and also swap the second and fourth, so this is a combination of two completely non-interacting transpositions, and as such is self-inverting.

As well as being a briefer way of writing permutations, the decomposed form is also more useful when assessing the order of a permutation.

KEY POINT 4.14

> The order of a permutation is the lcm (least common multiple) of the lengths of its decomposed *independent* cycles.

Note that when using this method to determine order, the cycles must be completely independent.

For example, $q = (13)(32)$ does not have order 2; the two cycles interact, since they share the element 3. In fact, $(13)(32) = (321)$ and so q has order 3.

Worked example 4.14

Determine the order of each of the following permutations on the set $\{1,2,3,4,5\}$:

$$p_1 = \begin{pmatrix} 1 & 2 & 3 & 4 & 5 \\ 4 & 3 & 2 & 5 & 1 \end{pmatrix} \quad p_2 = \begin{pmatrix} 1 & 2 & 3 & 4 & 5 \\ 2 & 1 & 4 & 3 & 5 \end{pmatrix} \quad p_3 = \begin{pmatrix} 1 & 2 & 3 & 4 & 5 \\ 1 & 5 & 2 & 4 & 3 \end{pmatrix} \quad p_4 = p_1 p_3$$

Decompose the permutations, and find the least common multiple of the cycle lengths

$$p_1 = (145)(23)$$
$\Rightarrow$ The order of p_1 is lcm$(2,3) = 6$
$$p_2 = (12)(34)$$
$\Rightarrow$ The order of p_2 is lcm$(2,2) = 2$
$$p_3 = (253)$$
$\Rightarrow$ The order of p_3 is 3

Resolve p_4 into a single permutation and then decompose that to establish its order

$$p_4 = \begin{pmatrix} 1 & 2 & 3 & 4 & 5 \\ 4 & 1 & 3 & 5 & 2 \end{pmatrix} = (1452)$$

$\Rightarrow$ The order of p_4 is 4.

EXAM HINT

The order of a composition of two permutations cannot be calculated as a function of the orders of the two initial permutations. First you must work out the composition as a single permutation and then assess its order.

If you are given permutations in cycle notation and asked to compose them, you need not transform back into the array to do so.

p_1 and p_2 are permutations on set $\{1,2,3,4,5\}$:

$p_1 = (123)$ $\qquad$ $p_2 = (1325)$

Express $p_2\, p_1$ as a single permutation.

Write the permutations out in order

$p_2 p_1 = (1325)\,(123)$

To resolve this, track each element in turn, completing a cycle when you return to an element already encountered
Start with 1:

$(15$

We see that that under the first cycle, 1 moves to 2, which moves under the second cycle to 5:
$1 \rightarrow 2 \rightarrow 5$

We now put 5 back in at the start (right side) and see what happens. 5 is unaffected by the first cycle and moves to 1 under the second. We have therefore come full circle and can close off the cycle

(15)

We have not yet finished however, since we have not investigated elements 2, 3 and 4.
Starting the next cycle with 2:
Under the first cycle, 2 moves to 3, which then moves back to 2. Thus 2 is unchanged by the permutation. We could write this as a 1-cycle (2), but would normally just disregard it. Starting the next cycle with 3:

Under the first cycle, 3 moves to 4, which is then unchanged. We now put 4 back in at the start (right side):

$(34$

4 moves to 1 under the first cycle, which moves to 3 under the second. We have therefore formed a second 2-cycle

(34)

We have now analysed all elements, so have finished. Although you do not need to show working for this sort of calculation, if you wish to do so as a means of making your answer easier for you to check, the following would be appropriate:

$\longrightarrow$

continued . . .

Write down the transformations, showing a
break at the end of a cycle
Always start the next line within a cycle with
the output of the previous line

Cycle analysis:
$$1 \to 2 \to 5]$$
$$5 \to 1]$$
$$2 \to 2]$$
$$3 \to 4]$$
$$4 \to 1 \to 3]$$

Read down the left hand column,
separating each cycle

$$p_2 p_1 = (15)(2)(34) = (15)(34)$$

EXAM HINT

Although we read left-to-right within each cycle, we take
the cycles in sequence from right to left. Take care not to
get confused by this effect!

Exercise 4E

1. Permutations p and q of the set $\{a,b,c,d,e\}$ are given by:

$$p = \begin{pmatrix} a & b & c & d & e \\ c & d & a & e & b \end{pmatrix} \qquad q = \begin{pmatrix} a & b & c & d & e \\ c & b & a & e & d \end{pmatrix}$$

   (a) Find the order of:

       (i) p (ii) q

   (b) (i) Find $p^{-1}q$.   (ii) Find the order of $p^{-1}q$.

2. The following are permutations of the set $\{1,2,3,4,5\}$:

$$p = \begin{pmatrix} 1 & 2 & 3 & 4 & 5 \\ 2 & 5 & 3 & 4 & 1 \end{pmatrix}$$

$$q = \begin{pmatrix} 1 & 2 & 3 & 4 & 5 \\ 3 & 1 & 2 & 4 & 5 \end{pmatrix}$$

$$r = \begin{pmatrix} 1 & 2 & 3 & 4 & 5 \\ 2 & 1 & 4 & 3 & 5 \end{pmatrix}$$

$$s = \begin{pmatrix} 1 & 2 & 3 & 4 & 5 \\ 5 & 2 & 4 & 1 & 3 \end{pmatrix}$$

   (a) Find permutations:

       (i) pr (ii) qs (iii) r^3 (iv) s^2

   (b) Find the order of:

       (i) p (ii) q (iii) r (iv) s

(c) Find the order of:

(i) pr (ii) qs (iii) r^3 (iv) s^2

(d) Find permutations:

(i) p^{-1} (ii) $(qr)^{-1}$ (iii) s^{-3} (iv) $p^{-1}rp$

3. Draw a square with vertices $(1,1),(-1,1),(-1,-1),(1,-1)$ and label the reflective symmetries. Using r for a rotation of $90°$ about the origin, draw out the group table for D_4.

4. P_4 represents the group of all permutations of the four letters a, b, c and d.

$p \in P_4$ is given by $p = \begin{pmatrix} a & b & c & d \\ c & a & b & d \end{pmatrix}$.

(a) Write down the identity element of P_4.

(b) Determine the order of p.

(c) It is given that $q^2 = p$. Find q.   [9 marks]

5. A $2 \times 2 \times 2$ puzzle cube consists of 8 blocks (A to H) around a central pivoting device. Each block has 3 external faces, as shown.

Labels have been assigned to each face according to its block and direction; the faces on the base are E_3, F_3, G_3 and H_3, the left side faces are A_1, B_1, F_1 and E_1 and the faces on the far side are B_2, C_2, G_2 and F_2.

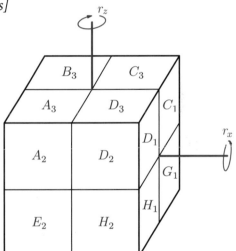

Rotations of four blocks are possible about the three axes connecting the centres of opposite faces.

We define a single $90°$ rotation of the upper layer through the vertical axis as $r_z = (A_1 B_2 C_1 D_2)(A_2 B_1 C_2 D_1)(A_3 B_3 C_3 D_3)$.

(a) Write down the full permutation of r_x, a rotation through $90°$ about the horizontal axis of the right four blocks, which contains the cycle $(C_1 D_1 H_1 G_1)$.

(b) Calculate the permutation $r_x^{-1} r_z^{-1} r_x r_z$.

(c) Interpret what effect the manoeuvre $r_x^{-1} r_z^{-1} r_x r_z$ has on the positions of the 8 blocks.

(d) Use your answer to (c) to describe what the effect would be of applying the manoeuvre twice in succession.

4F Homomorphisms and kernels

Homomorphisms

We know that there is an underlying structure common to all groups (closure, inverses, identity and associativity) but that, beyond these, groups can vary greatly. We now look at functions between groups.

Consider the groups:

$$\{A,*\} = \{\mathbb{Z}_8, \oplus_8\}, \text{ addition modulo } 8$$

and

$$\{B,\diamond\} = \{\mathbb{Z}_4, \oplus_4\}, \text{ addition modulo } 4$$

Function $f : A \to B$ is given by:

$$f(x) = \begin{cases} \dfrac{x}{2} & x \text{ even} \\ \dfrac{x-1}{2} & x \text{ odd} \end{cases}$$

We could alternatively write $f(x) = \left\lfloor \dfrac{x}{2} \right\rfloor$, using the floor brackets $\lfloor\ \rfloor$ which indicate 'round down to the nearest integer'.

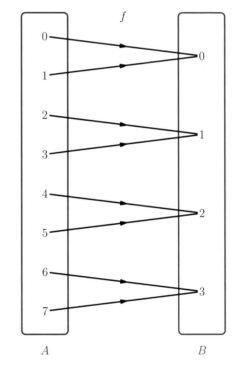

Function $g : A \to B$ is given by $g(x) = x \,(\text{modulo } 4)$

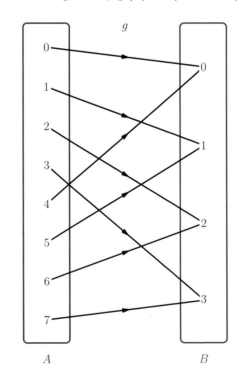

We can see that both functions f and g map all elements in $A = \{0,1,2,3,4,5,6,7\}$ to $B = \{0,1,2,3\}$ as required.

There is, however, a property of g which makes it mathematically far more interesting than f. We can illustrate the property by considering what happens when we apply each function to the following sum in A:

$$1 * 5$$

$$f(1 * 5) = f(6) = 3$$
$$\text{and } g(1 * 5) = g(6) = 2$$

If we were to map the original elements, prior to resolving the operation $*$:

$$f(1) = 0, f(5) = 2$$

and then (since $f(1)$ and $f(5)$ are elements of B), apply the operation of B:

$$f(1) \diamond f(5) = 0 \diamond 2 = 2$$

If we try the same with g, however: $\qquad g(1) = 1, g(5) = 1$

$$g(1) \diamond g(5) = 1 \diamond 1 = 2$$

It appears that if we apply f before resolving the group operation, we get a different result to applying f after the group operation, but with g we reached the same end either way:

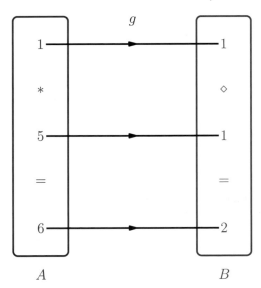

We could check that this effect will always hold true by testing every possible pair of elements from A, but that would require 27 more calculations. Better by far, we can use algebra to show the general case:

$$g(x * y) = g((x + y)(\text{modulo } 8)) = (x + y)(\text{modulo } 4)$$
$$g(x) \diamond g(y) = x(\text{modulo } 4) \diamond y(\text{modulo } 4) = (x + y)(\text{modulo } 4)$$

Thus:

$$g(x * y) = g(x) \diamond g(y)$$

for all $x, y \in A$.

Function g is called a **homomorphism** from A to B, because it 'preserves operations'.

This quality, where the structural relationships between elements of the domain group are preserved in the image elements of the range group, makes homomorphisms extraordinarily useful in group theory.

KEY POINT 4.15

> A homomorphism from group $\{A, *\}$ to group $\{B, \diamond\}$ is a function $f : A \to B$ such that $f(x * y) = f(x) \diamond f(y)$ for all elements $x, y \in A$.

Clearly g in the above example was not a bijection, since A has 8 elements and B has only 4. In fact, a homomorphism need not be injective or surjective; the only requirement is that it must preserve operations. The definition of homomorphism implies the following readily proved properties, which we can observe in the example.

First, we note that the identity element in A was 0, and this was mapped to the identity in B (also 0).

> **Property 1**
>
> If f is a group homomorphism from group $\{G, *\}$ to group $\{H, \diamond\}$ then the identity in G must be mapped to the identity in H:
> $$f(e_G) = e_H$$

Proof:

$g * e_G = g$ for all $g \in G$ (definition of e_G)

$\Rightarrow f(g * e_G) = f(g)$ for all $g \in G$

$\Rightarrow f(g) \diamond f(e_G) = f(g)$ for all $g \in G$ (definition of homomorphism)

$\Rightarrow f(g) \diamond f(e_G) = f(g) \diamond e_H$ for all $g \in G$ (definition of e_H)

$\therefore f(e_G) = e_H$ (left cancellation)

The inverse of 1 in A is 7. After applying the homomorphism, the images of these elements are also inverses:

$$g(1^{-1}) = g(7) = 3 = g(1)^{-1}$$

> **Property 2**
>
> If f is a group homomorphism from group $\{G, *\}$ to group $\{H, \diamond\}$ then the inverse of an element $g \in G$ must be mapped to the inverse of the image of g:
> $$f(g^{-1}) = f(g)^{-1} \text{ for all } g \in G$$

Proof:

$$g * g^{-1} = g^{-1} * g = e_G \text{ for all } g \in G \qquad \text{(definition of inverses)}$$

$$\Rightarrow f(g * g^{-1}) = f(g^{-1} * g) = f(e_G) = e_H \quad \text{(Corollary 1)}$$
for all $g \in G$

$$\Rightarrow f(g) \Diamond f(g^{-1}) = f(g^{-1}) \Diamond f(g) = e_H \qquad \text{(definition of}$$
for all $g \in G$ \qquad\qquad\qquad\qquad homomorphism)

$$\Rightarrow f(g^{-1}) = f(g)^{-1} \text{ for all } g \in G \qquad \text{(uniqueness of inverses)}$$

In fact, the homomorphism g preserved all powers, not just inverses.

Property 3

If f is a group homomorphism from group $\{G, *\}$ to group $\{H, \Diamond\}$ then the image of a power of an element is the same as the image of the element raised to that power:

$$f(g^n) = f(g)^n \text{ for all } g \in G, n \in \mathbb{Z}$$

Proof (by induction):

The case $n = 1$ is true.

Assume true for case $n = k$: \qquad\qquad\qquad (1)

$$f(g^k) = f(g)^k$$

Now:

$$f(g^{k+1}) = f(g * g^k) = f(g) \Diamond f(g^k) \qquad \text{(definition of}$$
\qquad\qquad\qquad\qquad\qquad\qquad\qquad homomorphism)

$$\Rightarrow \quad f(g^{k+1}) = f(g) \Diamond f(g)^k \qquad\qquad \text{(by (1))}$$

$$\Rightarrow \quad f(g^{k+1}) = f(g)^{k+1}$$

$\therefore f(g^n) = f(g)^n$ for all $n \in \mathbb{Z}^+$ by induction. \quad (2)

The case $n = 0$ is proved in Corollary 1 \qquad (3)

Since $g^{-n} = (g^{-1})^n$, the statement is also \qquad (by (2))
proved for $n \in \mathbb{Z}^-$:

$$f(g^{-n}) = f((g^{-1})^n) = f(g^{-1})^n \text{ for all } n \in \mathbb{Z}^+$$

$$\Rightarrow f(g^{-n}) = (f(g)^{-1})^n \text{ for all } n \in \mathbb{Z}^+ \qquad \text{(Corollary 2)}$$

$$\Rightarrow f(g^{-n}) = f(g)^{-n} \text{ for all } n \in \mathbb{Z}^+ \qquad (4)$$

$$f(g^n) = f(g)^n \text{ for all } n \in \mathbb{Z} \qquad \text{(by (2), (3), (4))}$$

Property 4

If f is a group homomorphism from group $\{G, *\}$ to group $\{H, \Diamond\}$ then the range of f will be a subgroup of H:

$$\{\{f(g) \mid g \in G\}, \Diamond\} \text{ is a subgroup of } \{H, \Diamond\}.$$

Proof:

Range of f contains the identity:

$$e_H = f(e_G) \in \{f(g) \mid g \in G\}$$

Closure follows from the definition of homomorphism and the closure of G.

Inverses follow from Property 2 and the presence of inverses in G.

Associativity is inherited from group H.

Worked example 4.16

Group $\{A, *\}$ is $\{0, 1, 2, 3, 4, 5\}$ under addition (modulo 6).

Group $\{B, \times\}$ is $\{1, -1\}$ under multiplication.

Functions f and g map A to B and are defined by:

$$f(x) = (-1)^x$$

$$g(x) = \begin{cases} 1 & x = 0, 1, 2 \\ -1 & x = 3, 4, 5 \end{cases}$$

Show that f is a homomorphism from A to B and that g is not.

We need to show that f preserves operations	$f(x * y) = f(x + y (\text{modulo } 6))$ $= (-1)^{x+y (\text{modulo } 6)}$ $= (-1)^{x+y}$ (difference of an even power would have no effect) $f(x) \times f(y) = (-1)^x \times (-1)^y = (-1)^{x+y}$ Hence $f(x * y) = f(x) \times f(y)$ So f is a group homomorphism from A to B
To show g is not a homomorphism we only need find one instance where operations are not preserved. We can see that $g(e_A) = e_B$, so try a non-identity element	$g(2 * 2) = g(4) = -1$ $g(2) \times g(2) = (-1) \times (-1) = 1$ Hence g does not preserve operations, and so is not a homomorphism from A to B.

Kernels

In Worked example 4.16,

Group $\{A, *\}$ is $\{0, 1, 2, 3, 4, 5\}$ under addition (modulo 6).

Group $\{B, \times\}$ is $\{1, -1\}$ under multiplication.

Homomorphism $f : A \rightarrow B$ is given by $f(x) = (-1)^x$.

We can partition A according to the image of each element in B, as shown in the diagram above.

Elements 0, 2 and 4 of A map to the identity element of B; this subset is called the **kernel** of homomorphism f, and, as we can quickly see, these elements form a subgroup of A.

KEY POINT 4.16

> For groups $\{G, *\}$ and $\{H, \diamond\}$ and group homomorphism $f : A \to B$, the kernel of f is defined as:
> $$\ker(f) = \{g \in G \mid f(g) = e_H\}$$
> $\ker(f)$ is a subgroup of $\{G, *\}$.

Worked example 4.17

For groups $\{G,*\}$ and $\{H,\diamond\}$, prove that the kernel of a group homomorphism $f:G\to H$ is a subgroup of G.

Define the kernel and use the definition of a homomorphism to demonstrate that all the group axioms are met

$\ker(f)=\{g\in G\,|\,f(g)=e_H\}$

Identity:

$f(e_G)=e_H$ (property of homomorphism)

$\therefore e_G\in\ker(f)$

Closure:

Suppose $g_1,g_2\in\ker(f)$.

$\Rightarrow f(g_1*g_2)=f(g_1)\diamond f(g_2)$ (definition of homomorphism)

$\Rightarrow f(g_1)*f(g_2)=e_H\diamond e_H=e_H$

$\Rightarrow g_1*g_2\in\ker(f)$

$\therefore \ker(f)$ is closed under $*$

Inverses:

Suppose $g\in\ker(f)$

$\Rightarrow f(g^{-1})=f(g)^{-1}$ (property of homomorphism)

$\Rightarrow f(g^{-1})=e_H^{-1}=e_H$

$\Rightarrow \therefore g^{-1}\in\ker(f)$

Associativity is inherited from the parent group

Therefore, $\ker(f)$ is a subgroup of $\{G,*\}$

Exercise 4F

1. (a) Which of the following functions f are homomorphisms from A to B?

   (i) $A=\{\mathbb{C}\backslash\{0\},\times\}$, $B=\{\mathbb{R}\backslash\{0\},\times\}$, $f(x)=|x|$

   (ii) $A=\{\mathbb{C},+\}$, $B=\{\mathbb{R},+\}$, $f(x)=|x|$

   (iii) $A=\{\mathbb{C}\backslash\{0\},\times\}$, $B=\{[0,2\pi[,+\}$, $f(x)=\arg(x)$

   where

   $$x*y=\begin{cases} x+y & x+y<2\pi \\ x+y-2\pi & \text{otherwise} \end{cases}$$

   (iv) $A=\{\mathbb{Z},+\}$, $B=\{\mathbb{Z},+\}$, $f(x)=5x$

   (b) For each part of (a) which describes a homomorphism, give $\ker(f)$.

2. f is a homomorphism from $\{\mathbb{Q},+\}$ to $\{\mathbb{C},+\}$ and $f(3)=2+\mathrm{i}$.

   (a) (i) State $f(0)$.

   (ii) Show that $f(n)=nf(1)$ for $n\in\mathbb{N}$. Hence find $f(1)$.

   (iii) Show that $f\!\left(\dfrac{1}{n}\right)=\dfrac{1}{n}f(1)$ for $n\in\mathbb{Z}^+$.

   (iv) Hence find an expression for $f(q)$ for $q\in\mathbb{Q}$.

   (b) State and prove whether f is injective, surjective or bijective.

3. f is a homomorphism from $\{G, *\}$ to $\{H, \diamond\}$.

Show that for any element $a \in G$:

$$\{g \in G \mid f(g) = f(a)\} = a * \ker(f) \qquad \text{[6 marks]}$$

4. f is a homomorphism from G to H.

Show that $\ker(f) = \{e_G\}$ if and only if f is injective. *[6 marks]*

5. Group $\{A, *\}$ is $\{0, 1, 2, 3, 4, 5, 6, 7\}$ under addition modulo 8.
Group $\{B, \diamond\}$ is $\{1, 3, 7, 9\}$ under multiplication modulo 10.

Homomorphism $f : A \to B$ is such that $f(1) = 7$.

(a) Find:

　　(i) $f(6)$　　　(ii) $\ker(f)$　　(iii) $\{a \in A \mid f(a) = 9\}$

Homomorphism $g : B \to A$ is such that $g(7) = 4$.

(b) Find:

　　(i) $\ker(g)$　　(ii) $\ker(g \circ f)$　　　*[12 marks]*

6. D_3 is given by the group table below:

$*$	e	r	s	x	y	z
e	e	r	s	x	y	z
r	r	s	e	z	x	y
s	s	e	r	y	z	x
x	x	y	z	e	r	s
y	y	z	x	s	e	r
z	z	x	y	r	s	e

Group $\{A, *\}$ is $\{0, 4\}$ under addition modulo 8.

Function $f : D_3 \to A$ is a group homomorphism from D_3 to A. Find all possible kernels of f and explain why there can be no others. *[9 marks]*

4G　Isomorphisms

Consider the following two groups:

$\{A, *\} = \{\mathbb{Z}_4, \oplus_4\}$, integers under addition (modulo 4)

$\{B, \diamond\} = \{\mathbb{Z}_5 \setminus \{0\}, \otimes_5\}$, non-zero integers under multiplication (modulo 5)

Although the elements and operations are different, these two examples have similar structures. Consider their Cayley tables:

The Cayley table for $\oplus_4$ in $\mathbb{Z}_4$:

$\oplus_4$	0	1	2	3
0	0	1	2	3
1	1	2	3	0
2	2	3	0	1
3	3	4	0	1

Element	Order
0	1 (0 is the identity)
1	4
2	2
3	4

The Cayley table for $\otimes_5$ in $\mathbb{Z}_5 \setminus \{0\}$:

$\otimes_5$	1	2	3	4
1	1	2	3	4
2	2	4	1	3
3	3	1	4	2
4	4	3	2	1

Element	Order
1	1 (1 is the identity)
2	4
3	4
4	2

As we can see that each of these groups has an element of order 4, and each group is itself order 4, we know (from Key point 4.5) that each must be a cyclic group:

$$\{\mathbb{Z}_4, \oplus_4\} = \;<1> \text{ and } \{\mathbb{Z}_5 \setminus \{0\}, \otimes_5\} = \;<2>$$

We could therefore express each of the groups in terms of its generator:

$*$	e	c	c^2	c^3
e	e	c	c^2	c^3
c	c	c^2	c^3	e
c^2	c^2	c^3	e	c
c^3	c^3	e	c	c^2

It should be clear that we can define a bijective homomorphism f from A to B by mapping a generator of A to a generator of B and then working through the other elements in terms of their powers. For example:

$$f(1) = 2$$
$$f(2) = f(1 \oplus_4 1) = f(1) \otimes_5 f(1) = 2 \otimes_5 2 = 4$$
$$f(3) = f(2 \oplus_4 1) = f(2) \otimes_5 f(1) = 4 \otimes_5 2 = 3$$
$$f(0) = f(e_A) = e_B = 1$$

KEY POINT 4.17

A homomorphism which is bijective is called an **isomorphism**.

For groups $\{G, *\}$ and $\{H, \circ\}$, where $n(G) = n(H)$, a bijective function $f : G \to H$ is an isomorphism if and only if:
$$f(g_1) \circ f(g_2) = f(g_1 * g_2) \text{ for all } g_1, g_2 \in G.$$

Two groups, between which an isomorphism exists, are said to be *isomorphic*.

Isomorphic groups have identical underlying structures. In addition to the properties of homomorphisms, we can demonstrate two more important features of isomorphisms which follow from the definition:

For groups $\{G, *\}$ and $\{H, \circ\}$, and isomorphism $f : G \to H$, the order of element $g \in G$ will always be equal to the order of its image $f(g) \in H$:

$$g^n = e_G \Leftrightarrow f(g)^n = e_H$$

Proof:

Suppose that element $g \in G$ has order divisible by n, so that $g^n = e_G$.

$\Leftrightarrow \quad f(g^n) = f(e_G) = e_H \qquad$ (property of homomorphism)

$\Leftrightarrow \quad f(g)^n = e_H \qquad\qquad$ (Corollary 3)

Property 2

For groups $\{G, *\}$ and $\{H, \circ\}$, and isomorphism $f : G \to H$, G is Abelian if and only if H is Abelian.

Proof:

Suppose that $g_1 * g_2 = g_2 * g_1$ for all $g_1, g_2 \in G$.

$\Leftrightarrow f(g_1 * g_2) = f(g_2 * g_1)$ for all $g_1, g_2 \in G$

$\Leftrightarrow f(g_1) \circ f(g_2) = f(g_2) \circ f(g_1)$ for all $g_1, g_2 \in G$ (property of homomorphism)

$\Leftrightarrow h_1 \circ h_2 = h_2 \circ h_1$ for all $h_1, h_2 \in H$ (f is a bijection)

The last step in this proof relies once again on the fact that f is a bijection, so:

$$H = \{f(g) \mid g \in G\}$$

that is, $f(g)$ can take all values in H, so that if something is true for $f(g)$ for all $g \in G$ then it must be true for all $h \in H$.

Additional property for cyclic groups

If G and H are both cyclic groups of the same order, with $G = <a>$ for some $a \in G$ and $H = <b>$ for some $b \in H$, then there is an isomorphism f such that $f(a^n) = b^n$ for all $n \in \mathbb{Z}$.

Worked example 4.18

Let $S = \left\{ a + b\sqrt{3} \mid a, b \in \mathbb{Q} \right\}$ and $f : S \to S$ be a function given by:
$$f\left(a + b\sqrt{3}\right) = a - b\sqrt{3}$$

It is given that S forms a group under standard multiplication. Show that f is an isomorphism from $\{S, \times\}$ to $\{S, \times\}$.

Show that f is injective

Suppose $f\left(a + b\sqrt{3}\right) = f\left(c + d\sqrt{3}\right)$

$\Rightarrow a - b\sqrt{3} = c - d\sqrt{3}$

$\Rightarrow a = c, b = d$

$\therefore f$ is injective

continued . . .

Show that f is injective

Then show that f is a homomorphism (preserves operations)

For all $a, b \in Q$,

$a + b\sqrt{3} = f(a - b\sqrt{3})$

where $a - b\sqrt{3} \in S$

∴ f is surjective

∴ f is bijective

$\left(a + b\sqrt{3}\right)\left(c + d\sqrt{3}\right) = \left(ac + 3bd\right) + \left(bc + ad\right)\sqrt{3}$

$\Rightarrow f\left(\left(a + b\sqrt{3}\right)\left(c + d\sqrt{3}\right)\right) = \left(ac + 3bd\right)\;\left(bc + ad\right)\sqrt{3}$

and

$f\left(a + b\sqrt{3}\right) \times f\left(c + d\sqrt{3}\right) = \left(a - b\sqrt{3}\right)\left(c - d\sqrt{3}\right)$

$= \left(ac + 3bd\right) - \left(bc + ad\right)\sqrt{3}$

∴ $f\left(\left(a + b\sqrt{3}\right) \times \left(c + d\sqrt{3}\right)\right) = f\left(a + b\sqrt{3}\right) \times f\left(c + d\sqrt{3}\right)$

∴ f is a bijection which preserves operations, and hence is an isomorphism.

EXAM HINT

In this worked example, we proved isomorphism with algebra. For small groups, it is often easiest to prove that two groups are isomorphic by recognising their common group structure as one of the specified few in Section 4E. It is not sufficient simply to show that two groups have the same order structure.

Exercise 4G

1. Define an isomorphism between two groups, $\{G, *\}$ and $\{H, \circ\}$.

2. Isomorphism f maps cyclic group G to group H. Show that H must be cyclic.

3. A relation R on the set S of all groups is defined as:

   $GRH \Leftrightarrow G$ is isomorphic to H

   Prove that R is an equivalence relation.

4. Show that function $f : x \mapsto \ln x$ is an isomorphism from $\{\mathbb{R}^+, \times\}$ to $\{\mathbb{R}, +\}$. *[4 marks]*

5. (a) Set A contains the elements $7, 7^2, 7^3, 7^4, 7^5, 7^6$, written modulo 36.

   Show that A forms a group under multiplication (modulo 36), and determine the order of each of the elements.

   (b) Find an isomorphism between the group from part (a) and the group $\{0, 1, 2, 3, 4, 5\}$ under addition modulo 6. *[8 marks]*

6. The following are permutations of the set $\{1,2,3,4,5\}$:

$$p_1 = \begin{pmatrix} 1 & 2 & 3 & 4 & 5 \\ 2 & 5 & 3 & 4 & 1 \end{pmatrix}$$

$$p_2 = \begin{pmatrix} 1 & 2 & 3 & 4 & 5 \\ 1 & 2 & 3 & 4 & 5 \end{pmatrix}$$

$$p_3 = \begin{pmatrix} 1 & 2 & 3 & 4 & 5 \\ 2 & 5 & 4 & 3 & 1 \end{pmatrix}$$

$$p_4 = \begin{pmatrix} 1 & 2 & 3 & 4 & 5 \\ 5 & 1 & 3 & 4 & 2 \end{pmatrix}$$

(a) Give two more permutations p_5 and p_6 so that
$P = \{p_1, p_2, p_3, p_4, p_5, p_6\}$ form a group under composition
of permutations, and draw out the group table.

(b) State, giving your reason, whether P is isomorphic to D_3 or
to the cyclic group of order 6. *[10 marks]*

7. $\{G, *\}$ is a non-Abelian group, with $g \in G$.
Function $f : G \to G$ is defined by:

$$f : x \mapsto g^{-1} * x * g$$

Show that f is an isomorphism from G to itself. *[6 marks]*

8. Groups $\{G, *\}$ and $\{A, \circ\}$ are isomorphic, with isomorphism
$f : G \to A$.

H is a subgroup of G. Prove that the image of H under f will
form a subgroup of A. *[6 marks]*

9. $\{\mathbb{R} \setminus \{0\}, \times\}$ and $\{\mathbb{R}^+, \times\}$ are both non-cyclic, Abelian,
infinite groups. Explain why neither of the following can be
isomorphisms between them:

(a) $f : x \mapsto |x|$

(b) $f : x \mapsto 2^{x-1}$ *[4 marks]*

10. The set of symmetries of a non-square rhombus is
$S = \{D, d, r, e\}$, where:

D represents reflection through the longer diagonal

d represents reflection through the shorter diagonal

r represents a rotation of π about the centre

e represents a rotation of 0 about the centre

(a) Write down the table of operations for S under $\circ$, the
composition of transformations.

(b) Assuming $\circ$ is associative, show that S forms a group
under $\circ$.

(c) State, with justification, whether $\{S, \circ\}$ is isomorphic to
$\{\{1, -1, i, -i\}, \times\}$. *[10 marks]*

11. (a) Show that set $A = \{1, 5, 7, 11\}$ forms a group under $\otimes_{12}$, multiplication (modulo 12).

(b) Function $f: \mathbb{Z}_4 \to \mathbb{Z}$ is given as $f(x) = 5 - 13x + 11x^2 - 2x^3$.

Show that f is a bijection from $\mathbb{Z}_4$ to A and establish whether it is an isomorphism between groups $\{\mathbb{Z}_4, \oplus_4\}$ and $\{A, \otimes_{12}\}$.

[8 marks]

12. Set F_n is defined for any positive integer n as:
$$F_n = \{x \in \mathbb{Z}^+ \mid x < n, \gcd(x, n) = 1\}$$

(a) Show that F_n forms a group under multiplication (modulo n).

(b) Determine which of groups F_5, F_8, F_{10} and F_{12} are isomorphic.

[10 marks]

Summary

- In this chapter we introduced the concept of a group, and investigated properties of groups and subgroups, with specific reference to groups of functions, permutations, symmetries and integers modulo n.

- A **group** is any set A together with a binary operator $*$ such that:

  - $a * b \in A$ for all $a, b \in A$ (A is closed under $*$).

  - $e \in A$ (A contains the identity of $*$).

  - For all $a \in A, a^{-1} \in A$ (A contains inverses for all its elements).

  - $a * (b * c) = (a * b) * c$ for all $a, b, c \in A$ ($*$ is associative in A).

- A group which is also commutative is called an **Abelian group**.

- For group $\{G, *\}$, $n(G)$ is the number of elements of G, called the **order** of G.

- A **cyclic group** has a **generator** element, so that every element of the group can be expressed as a power of the generator.

- $\{H, *\}$ is a **subgroup** of a group $\{G, *\}$ when $H \subseteq G$ and $\{H, *\}$ fulfils the group axioms; associativity can always be assumed to be inherited.

- **Lagrange's theorem** states that for any subgroup H of a group G, $n(H)$ divides $n(G)$.

  - the order of any element will divide the order of a group containing it.

  - a prime order group will be cyclic, with every non-identity element as generator.

- Simple group structures:

  - Any prime order group must be cyclic (C_p).

  - An order 4 group may be cyclic (C_4) or **Klein-four**.

  - An order 6 group may be cyclic (C_6) or isomorphic to D_3.

- **Symmetries** of a 2-dimensional figure, expressed as rotations and reflections, form a group under composition. For a regular n-gon, the group is called D_n, the **dihedral group of order** n.

- Permutations of a list of elements form a group under composition.

- Decomposition of a permutation into independent cycles is useful for determining order.

- A **homomorphism** is a function mapping one group to another which preserves operations, so that for $f:\{G,*\}\rightarrow\{H,\circ\}$:

$$f(g_1 * g_2) = f(g_1) \circ f(g_2)$$
$$f(e_G) = f(e_H)$$
$$f(g^n) = f(g)^n$$

- The **kernel** of a homomorphism is that subgroup of the domain which maps to the identity element of the codomain group.

$$\ker(f) = \{g \in G \mid f(g) = e_H\}$$

- An **isomorphism** is a bijective homomorphism:

  - isomorphic groups have identical group structures

  - isomorphisms preserve element order.

Mixed examination practice 4

1. Prove that the set $\{3n \mid n \in \mathbb{Z}\}$ forms a group under addition.

2. Consider sets $G = \{1, 9, 11, 19\}$ and $H = \{1, 3, 7, 9\}$ under multiplication modulo 20.
   (a) Draw a Cayley table for each set.
   (b) Prove that both G and H are groups.
   (c) Write down the inverse of the element 9:
       (i) in G (ii) in H
   (d) State, with a reason, whether H and G are isomorphic.

3. Let $F = \{1, 2, 3, 4\}$ and let $\otimes_5$ denote multiplication modulo 5.
   (a) Show that $(F, \otimes_5)$ is a group and list the orders of all the elements.
   (b) State, with a reason, whether $(F, \otimes_5)$ is a cyclic group.

4. Operation $\ast$ is defined on $\mathbb{R}^2$ by:
   $$(a, b) \ast (x, y) = (a + x - by, b + y)$$
   Show that $\mathbb{R}^2$ forms a group under $\ast$.   *[6 marks]*

5. Show that every cyclic group of order at least three has at least two generator elements.   *[6 marks]*

6. Functions $\{p, q, r, s\}$ are defined on $\mathbb{R} \setminus \{1\}$, and:
   $$p(x) = x$$
   $$q(x) = \frac{x - 2}{x - 1}$$
   $$r(x) = 2 - x$$
   (a) Given $\{p, q, r, s\}$ form a group under composition of functions, find s.
   (b) Show that $q^2 = p$ and that q and r commute.
   (c) Draw the group table.   *[9 marks]*

7. Relation $\lozenge$ is defined on $\mathbb{C} \setminus \{0\}$ by:
   $$w \lozenge z \text{ if and only if } \arg(w) = \arg(z)$$
   (a) Show that $\lozenge$ is an equivalence relation on $\mathbb{C} \setminus \{0\}$ and partitions it into classes A_θ given by:
   $$A_\theta = \{a \operatorname{cis}(\theta) \mid a \in \mathbb{R}^+\}$$
   Operation $\ast$ is defined on $\mathbb{C}$ by $w \ast z = |wz| \operatorname{cis}\left(\frac{\arg(w) + \arg(z)}{2}\right)$.
   (b) Show that A_θ forms a group under $\ast$.
   (c) Find the image of A_θ under function $f : z \mapsto \dfrac{1}{z}$ and show that f is an isomorphism between the two groups.   *[10 marks]*

8. Group $\{G, *\}$ has subset H such that:
$$H = \{g \in G \mid g * a = a * g \text{ for all } a \in G\}$$
Show that H is a subgroup of G. **[6 marks]**

9. Group G of order 8 with operation $*$ has elements $\{e, p, p^2, p^3, q, qp, qp^2, qp^3\}$, where qp is taken to mean $q * p$.

It is known that $p^2 = q^2 = (qp)^2$.

(a) Show that $p^4 = e$.

(b) Show that $p = qpq$ and $q = pqp$.

(c) Determine whether G is Abelian. **[8 marks]**

10. Let a, b and p be elements of a group $(H, *)$ with an identity element e.

(a) If element a has order n and element a^{-1} has order m, then prove that $m = n$.

(b) If $b = p^{-1} * a * p$, prove, by mathematical induction, that $b^m = p^{-1} * a^m * p$, where $m = 1, 2, \ldots$. **[9 marks]**

(© IB Organization 2000)

11. Shown below are the operation tables for two isomorphic groups G and H.

$*$	a	b	c	d
a	d	a	b	c
b	a	b	c	d
c	b	c	d	a
d	c	d	a	b

$\circ$	2	4	6	8
2	4	8	2	6
4	8	6	4	2
6	2	4	6	8
8	6	2	8	4

(a) Function f is an isomorphism from G to H. Give all possible values of $f(a)$, $f(b)$, $f(c)$ and $f(d)$.

(b) Give a possible operation represented by $\circ$. **[6 marks]**

12. G is a cyclic group of order 12 with identity e and an element r such that r^4 has order 3.

(a) Write down the possible orders for r.

(b) Given that the order of r^{12} is less than the order of r^6, write down in terms of r the elements of an order 4 subgroup H of G. **[8 marks]**

13. An element g of a group G is said to be 'asymmetric' if:
$$g * x = x * g \Rightarrow x = g, x = e \text{ or } g = e$$
Show that a group, all of whose elements are asymmetric, can have order no greater than 2. **[4 marks]**

14. Consider the set $U = \{1, 3, 5, 9, 11, 13\}$ under the operation $*$, where $*$ is multiplication modulo 14. (In all parts of this problem, the general properties of multiplication modulo n may be assumed.)

(a) Show that $(3 * 9) * 13 = 3 * (9 * 13)$.

(b) Show that $(U, *)$ is a group.

(c) (i) Define a cyclic group.

    (ii) Show that $(U, *)$ is cyclic and find all its generators.

(d) Show that there are only two non-trivial proper subgroups of this group, and find them.

                                                                  (29 marks)

                                              (© *IB Organization 1999*)

15. $G = \{e, a, a^2, a^3, b, b*a, b*a^2, b*a^3\}$ forms a non-Abelian group of order 8 under operation $*$.

(a) Show that a has order 4.

(b) Show that $b^2 = a^2$ or e.

(c) If $b^2 = e$, show that G is isomorphic to D_4.

(d) Assuming $b^2 = a^2$:

    (i)   show that $b*a^3 = a*b$.

    (ii) find three subgroups of G of order 4.   *[10 marks]*

16. $A = \{2^n \,(\text{modulo}\,15) \mid n \in \mathbb{N}\}$

$$B = \left\{ \text{cis}\left(\frac{n\pi}{2}\right) \text{ for } n \in \{0, 1, 2, 3\} \right\}$$

(a) Show that B forms a group under multiplication.

(b) Write down the operation table for A under multiplication (modulo 15).

(c) Write down the order of each element of A.

(d) $f(x) = e^{i\frac{\pi}{2}\log_2 x}$. Show that f is an isomorphism from A to B.   *[10 marks]*

17. G is the set of permutations $\{A, B, C, D\}$, where:

$$A = \begin{pmatrix} 1 & 2 & 3 & 4 \\ 4 & 3 & 2 & 1 \end{pmatrix}, \quad B = \begin{pmatrix} 1 & 2 & 3 & 4 \\ 1 & 2 & 3 & 4 \end{pmatrix}$$

$$C = \begin{pmatrix} 1 & 2 & 3 & 4 \\ 3 & 1 & 4 & 2 \end{pmatrix}, \quad D = \begin{pmatrix} 1 & 2 & 3 & 4 \\ 2 & 4 & 1 & 3 \end{pmatrix}$$

(a) Draw the Cayley table for G under $*$ (composition of permutations) and show that $\{G, *\}$ forms a group.

(b) Identify a set $S \subset \mathbb{Z}$ and an operation $\circ$ such that $\{G, *\}$ is isomorphic to $\{S, \circ\}$.   *[10 marks]*

5 Summary and mixed examination practice

Introductory problem revisited

An automated shuffling machine separates a deck of n cards in half, leaving the extra card in the lower half if n is odd, inverts the lower half and then exactly interleaves the two, so that an ordered deck of cards labelled 1, 2, 3, ..., n would, after one shuffle, be in the order $n, 1, (n-1), 2, (n-2), 3,\ldots$

The machine is used on a deck of seven cards.

After how many shuffles would the deck have returned to its original order?

Would it be possible to use the machine to exactly reverse a deck of n cards? If so, for what values of n?

We can interpret this as a permutation p_n on n cards. In the first case, where $n = 7$, we see that the permutation is:

$$p_7 = \begin{pmatrix} 7 & 1 & 6 & 2 & 5 & 3 & 4 \\ 1 & 2 & 3 & 4 & 5 & 6 & 7 \end{pmatrix} = (7124)(63)$$

(Notice that the description of the permutation told us the source of cards in the new arrangement rather than the destination of each card in the original arrangement, hence the slightly strange ordering.)

This permutation has order lcm $(4, 2) = 4$, so if repeated 4 times (or any multiple of 4 times), it will restore the deck to its original state.

The question about the general case requires more subtlety. We are asked whether, for:

$$p_n = \begin{pmatrix} n & 1 & n-1 & 2 & \ldots & \lceil n/2 \rceil \\ 1 & 2 & 3 & 4 & \ldots & n \end{pmatrix}$$

and reverse ordering:

$$r = \begin{pmatrix} n & n-1 & n-2 & n-3 & \ldots & 1 \\ 1 & 2 & 3 & 4 & \ldots & n \end{pmatrix}$$

there is some value k such that:

$$(p_n)^k = r$$

(The upper brackets $\lceil\ \rceil$ are a shorthand notation for the 'ceiling' function, which returns the smallest integer value greater than or equal to the value in the brackets. So $\lceil 4 \rceil = 4$ and $\lceil 2.5 \rceil = 3$. Similarly, lower brackets $\lfloor\ \rfloor$ denote the 'floor' function which returns the greatest integer value less than or equal to the value in the brackets. Using these, we avoid having to separate the working for the two cases, n odd and n even.)

The decomposition of r gives multiple 2-cycles

$$r = (1\ n)(2\ (n-1))...(\lfloor n/2 \rfloor\ \lceil n/2 \rceil)$$

whereas the decomposition of p_n contains the cycle $c = (n\ 1\ 2\ 4...\lceil n/2 \rceil)$.

It follows that if $(p_n)^k$ is required to map $n \rightarrow 1$, it must contain c as given above, and no power of c which is not itself equal to c (since any other power of c will map n to an element other than 1).

But c maps 1 to 2.

So if $(p_n)^k$ is required to contain the transposition $(1\ n)$ then $n = 2$.

Hence the only deck size which can be exactly reversed by the protocol described is a deck of size 2.

Summary

This Option covers abstract concepts of operations, relations and groups, which generalise familiar algebraic ideas. To build up these concepts we need a good understanding of sets. An operation is a way of combining two elements of a set to get a result (for example, adding two numbers produces another number) and a relation is a rule that two elements may or may not satisfy (such as being equal). In this Option we concentrated on properties of operations and relations themselves, rather than on the particular elements on which they act. Of special interest is the concept of a group, which is a set with an operation with certain properties that allow us perform calculations similar to those of basic algebra. Once we know the structure of a group (such as the orders of all the elements and possible subgroups), we can derive conclusions about its elements without worrying about what those elements are. This means that if two groups have the same structure (such groups are called isomorphic) we can use our knowledge of one group to make conclusions about the other. Thus abstract calculations can lead to results about concrete objects.

In chapter 2 of this option, we examined the structure and rules surrounding sets in a formal way and encountered the algebraic concept of a binary operation, which combines two elements of a set under a defined rule to produce a new element.

You should know about:

- Sets and notation for their description, size, exclusions and subsets.

- Operations on sets and the qualities of closure, associativity, commutativity and distributivity for operations.

- The concept of identity and inverse elements for a given operation.

- Set operations of union, intersection, set difference and symmetric difference, and the interactions between them.

- Distributivity of union with intersection and the interaction of complement with union and intersection (De Morgan's laws).

In chapter 3 of this option, we introduced the concept of ordered pairs and the Cartesian product of two sets; we then considered relations and finally functions as subsets of Cartesian products, under specified restrictions.

You should know about:

- The Cartesian product of two sets and how to interpret ordered pairs.

- Relations as subsets of Cartesian products, the concepts of domain and range for a relation and the qualities of reflexivity, symmetry and transitivity for relations.

- Equivalence relations, equivalence classes and the specific example of numerical congruence modulo n as an equivalence relation on integers.

- Functions as restricted examples of relations, the concepts of domain, range and codomain for a function and the qualities of injectivity, surjectivity and bijectivity for functions.

- Composition of functions, the inverse of a bijective function and how to determine these.

In chapter 4 of this option, we introduced the concept of a group, and investigated properties of groups and subgroups, with specific reference to groups of functions, permutations, symmetries and integers modulo n.

You should know about:

- The four axioms of a group and the additional requirement for an Abelian group.

- Cyclic groups and their generator elements.

- Lagrange's theorem and its corollaries which show how the order of a group can be used to provide information on the orders of elements and subgroups.

- The structures of small groups, specifically cyclic groups, the Klein 4-group and the dihedral group D_3.

- Examples of groups: Functions, symmetries of plane figures and permutations.

- Homomorphisms as functions between groups which preserve operations.

- Homomorphism kernel as the subgroup of elements of the domain group which are mapped to the identity of the codomain group.

- Isomorphisms as bijective homomorphisms between groups of identical structure.

Mixed examination practice 5

1. Show that the set $T = \{a + b\sqrt{3} \,|\, a, b \in \mathbb{Z}\}$ forms a group under addition.

   [4 marks]

2. The relation R is defined on the set of complex numbers by $z_1 R z_2 \Leftrightarrow |z_1| = |z_2|$.

   (a) Show that R is an equivalence relation.

   C_1 denotes the equivalence class containing i.

   (b) Describe C_1 on an Argand diagram.

   (c) Show that C_1 forms a group under multiplication.   [8 marks]

3. Consider the set $G = \{1, 3, 5, 9, 11, 13\}$ under multiplication modulo 14.

   (a) Construct a Cayley table for G.

   (b) Given that G is a group,

      (i) Find the order of each element.

      (ii) Write down the inverse of 9.

      (iii) Find a subgroup of order 3.   [8 marks]

4. In this question, U denotes the universal set and $\mathcal{M}$ denotes the set of all subsets of U.

   (a) For a set $A \in \mathcal{M}$, write down $A \cap U$ and $A \cap \varnothing$.

   (b) Use Venn diagrams to illustrate that the operation $\cap$ is associative.

   (c) Explain why $\{\mathcal{M}, \cap\}$ is not a group, stating clearly which groups axiom is not satisfied.   [7 marks]

5. Operation $*$ on $\mathbb{R}$ is defined by $x * y = x + y - a$ where $a \in \mathbb{R}$ is a fixed constant.

   (a) Prove that $\mathbb{R}$ forms a group under $*$.

   (b) State, with proof, whether the group is Abelian.

   (c) Prove that there are no elements of order 2.

   (d) Show that $\mathbb{R}^+$ does not form a group under $*$.   [12 marks]

6. The operation $*$ on $\mathbb{R}$ is defined by:
   $$x * y = x|y|$$

   (a) Show that $*$ is not commutative.

   (b) Show that $*$ is associative.

   (c) Determine whether $\mathbb{R}$ forms a group under $*$.   [8 marks]

7. For each of the following groups, write down the minimum possible order of the group, giving your reason.

(a) Group A is cyclic and has a proper subgroup.

(b) Group B has a proper subgroup of order 3.

(c) Group C has three proper subgroups. *[6 marks]*

8. A group G with identity e contains two distinct non-identity elements a and b, such that:

$$a^7 = e$$

$$a^{-1}ba = a^5b$$

(a) Show that $b = aba$.

(b) Prove that $b = a^n ba^n$ for any $n \in \mathbb{N}$. *[6 marks]*

9. Function f is defined on $\mathbb{R} \setminus \{0,1,k\}$ by

$$f : x \mapsto \frac{1}{2-2x}$$

Function g is given by $g(x) = ff(x)$.

(a) Find $g(x)$ and $gg(x)$.

(b) State value k such that f is bijective on $\mathbb{R} \setminus \{0,1,k\}$.

(c) K is a group of order 4 of functions on $\mathbb{R} \setminus \{0,1,k\}$ under composition, with $f, g \in K$. Find the other two elements e and h of K and construct the group table. *[12 marks]*

10. Let R_n be the relation on $\mathbb{Z}$ 'congruence (modulo n)'.

(a) Prove that R_n is an equivalence relation on $\mathbb{Z}$.

(b) Prove that R_n partitions $\mathbb{Z}$ into n distinct classes.

(c) Let $\mathbb{Z}_n$ be the set of all the equivalence classes found in (b). Define a suitable binary operation $*_m$ on $\mathbb{Z}_m$ and prove that $\{\mathbb{Z}_m, *_m\}$ is an additive Abelian group.

(d) Let $\{G, \circ\}$ be a cyclic group of order n. Prove that $\{G, \circ\}$ is isomorphic to $\{\mathbb{Z}_m, *_m\}$. *[17 marks]*

11. Consider the group G defined on the set $S = \{1, 2, 4, 5, 7, 8\}$ having the following Cayley table.

$*$	1	2	4	5	7	8
1	1	2	4	5	7	8
2	2	4	8	1	5	7
4	4	8	7	2	1	5
5	5	1	2	7	8	4
7	7	5	1	8	4	2
8	8	7	5	4	2	1

(a) Explain what is meant by saying that this table is a Latin square.

(b) Solve the equation

$$2 * x * 7 = 4 \text{ where } x \in S.$$

(c) (i) Show that G is cyclic and find the generators.

    (ii) List the proper subgroups of G. [15 marks]

(© IB Organization 2006)

A group G of order 9 contains distinct elements x and y each of order 3 with $x \neq y^2$. The identity is given as e, and the result of the group operation on elements a and b is denoted ab.

(a) Write down the elements of a proper subgroup which does not contain x.

(b) Find the order of xy.

(c) Express $(xy)^2$ as a product of two of the elements x, y, x^2 and y^2 and hence show that $xy = yx$.

(d) Hence prove that the group is Abelian and list the elements in simplest form. [15 marks]

13. The group $(G, \times)$ has a subgroup $(H, \times)$. The relation R is defined on G by

$$(x \, R \, y) \Leftrightarrow (x^{-1}y \in H), \text{ for } x, y \in G.$$

(a) Show that R is an equivalence relation.

(b) Given that $G = \{e, p, p^2, q, pq, p^2q\}$, where e is the identity element, $p^3 = q^2 = e$ and $qp = p^2q$, prove that $qp^2 = pq$.

(c) Given also that $H = \{e, p^2q\}$, find the equivalence class with respect to R which contains pq. [16 marks]

(© IB Organization 2005)

Supplementary sheet: Groups of order 6

We can find all group structures of order 4, by using the method demonstrated in Section 4E. We can determine all possible structures for groups of order 6 by consideration of Lagrange's theorem and construction of Cayley tables.

By Lagrange's theorem, each element must have order 1, 2, 3 or 6.

If any element has order 6, then the group must be cyclic C_6, isomorphic to $\{\mathbb{Z}_6, \oplus_6\}$.

Alternatively, suppose that there is no element of order 6.

Suppose element a has order 3.

Then the group contains elements e, a and a^2 and must contain also another element b distinct from these, and hence (by closure) also $b * a$ and $b * a^2$.

Partially construct a Cayley table using these details:

$*$	e	a	a^2	b	$b * a$	$b * a^2$
e						
a						
a^2						
b						
$b * a$						
$b * a^2$						

There is not yet sufficient here to uniquely determine the remaining cells of the table according to the Latin square requirement, but we can use a reasoned argument based on inverses.

Consider which element could represent b^{-1}:

We already know that $b * e \neq e$, $b * a \neq e$ and $b * a^2 \neq e$.

If $b * (b * a) = e$ then, by associativity, $b^2 * a = e$

$\Rightarrow$ (by uniqueness of inverses), $b^2 = $ _____ $\neq e$

and also $b^3 = b * a^2 \neq e$.

So b cannot have order 2 or 3, and hence by Lagrange must have order 6, which contradicts our initial requirement.

By exactly the same logic, if $b * (b * a^2) = e$ then we find again that b must have order 6.

The only way we can construct a non-cyclic group is to require that $b^{-1} = b$, so that b has order 2. Equivalent arguments can be used to show that $b * a$ and $b * a^2$ must also be self-inverse. We can then complete the Cayley table using associativity and the Latin square principle.

$*$	e	a	a^2	b	$b * a$	$b * a^2$
e						
a						
a^2						
b						
$b * a$						
$b * a^2$						

Finally we consider the case where a group of order 6 only has elements of order 2.

We know that any such group must be Abelian (See Worked example 4.5). Then $\{e, a, b, a * b\}$ will be closed under $*$ and form a Klein subgroup within the group. Since by Lagrange's theorem no group of order 6 could have a subgroup of order 4, we conclude that there can be no group of order 6, all elements of which are self-inverse.

Thus there are only two possible structures for groups of order 6: The cyclic group with order structure 1, 2, 3, 3, 6, 6 and this second structure, denoted D_3 (D_6 in some texts), called the 'dihedral group of order 3', which has order structure 1, 2, 2, 2, 3, 3.

D_3 is the smallest non-Abelian group, since cyclic groups and the Klein group are all Abelian.

Answers

Chapter 1

Exercise 1A

1. Assume that n^2 is even but n is odd, and consider $n \times n$.
2. Assume that there are such numbers and factorise the expression.
3. Assume that $\log_2 5 = \dfrac{p}{q}$ and rearrange this expression to get even = odd.
4. Suppose that L is the largest even integer and consider $L + 2$.
5. If this was not true, all of them would be under 18; what can you say about the average?
6. Assume that $a + b = c$ where a and c are rational and b is irrational, and consider $c - a$.
7. Assume that $\hat{C} \neq 90°$, and consider two possible cases: $\hat{C} < 90°$ and $\hat{C} > 90°$. In each case draw a perpendicular line from C and apply Pythagoras to the resulting triangle.
8. (a) -0.682
   (b) Write $x = \dfrac{p}{q}$ and show that p and q must both be even.

Chapter 2

Exercise 2A

1. (a) (i) a,b,c,d (ii) $2,4,6,8$
   (b) (i) a,e,i,o,u (ii) $2,3,5,7$
   (c) (i) $0,1,2,3,4$ (ii) $2,-2$
   (d) (i) $-4,-3,-2,-1,4$
       (ii) $0,1,i,-1,-i$
   (e) (i) $1,3,5,7,9$
       (ii) $-6,-3,0,3,6$

2. (a) (i) 4   (ii) 2
   (b) (i) 0   (ii) 1
   (c) (i) 12   (ii) 50
   (d) (i) 7
       (ii) ∞ (infinite set)
   (e) (i) 6   (ii) 7

3. (a) $\mathbb{Q}, \mathbb{R}$ (b) None
   (c) $\mathbb{N}, \mathbb{Z}, \mathbb{Q}, \mathbb{R}$ (d) $\mathbb{Q}, \mathbb{R}$

4. (a) $A \subset B$, e.g. $-1 \in B, -1 \notin A$
   (b) $A = B$
   (c) $A \supset B$, eg $\pi \in A, \pi \notin B$
   (d) $A \subset B$. $\varnothing \in B$

5. (a) $\{\varnothing, \{0\}, \{1\}, \{0,1\}\}$
   (b) $\left\{ \begin{array}{c} \varnothing, \{a\}, \{b\}, \{c\}, \{d\}, \\ \{a,b\}, \{a,c\}, \{a,d\}, \{b,c\}, \{b,d\}, \{c,d\}, \\ \{a,b,c\}, \{a,b,d\}, \{a,c,d\}, \{b,c,d\}, \\ \{a,b,c,d\} \end{array} \right\}$

Exercise 2B

1. (a) (i) 4   (ii) -11
       (iii) 0   (iv) 15
   (c) (i) $x = 5$ (ii) $x = -2$

2. (a) A, B   (b) A
   (c) B, C   (d) B, C

3. (a) (i) $e = -1$, $x^{-1} = -x - 2$
       (ii) $e = \dfrac{1}{2}$, $x^{-1} = \dfrac{1}{4x}$, $x \neq 0$
   (b) (i) No identity   (ii) $e = 0$, $v^{-1} = -v$
   (c) (i) $e = 0$, $x^{-1} = x$ (ii) No identity

4. (a)

$*$	0	1	2	3
0	0	1	2	3
1	1	1	1	1
2	2	1	0	1
3	3	1	1	3

Closed, $e = 0$

   (b)

$*$	0	2	4	6
0	0	0	0	0
2	0	1	2	3
4	0	2	4	6
6	0	3	6	9

Not closed, $e = 4$

   (c)

$*$	7	8	9
7	7	8	9
8	8	8	9
9	9	9	9

Closed, $e = 7$

5. (a) (i) Yes   (ii) Yes
       (iii) No   (iv) Yes
   (b) (i) Yes   (ii) Yes
   (c) (i) No   (ii) No
   (d) (i) No identity in $\mathbb{Z}^+$
       (ii) $e = 2$
   (e) (i) $x^{-1} = x$ for all $x \in \mathbb{Z}$
       (ii) $x^{-1} = \dfrac{x}{x-1}$ for all $x \in \mathbb{Z} \setminus \{1\}$

7. (a) Closed for $k \le 1$ (b) Commutative
(c) Associative   (d) $e = k$
(e) $\{x \in \mathbb{Z}^+ \mid x < 2k\}$

8. (b) (i) 0   (ii) 1   (iii) 2

Exercise 2C

1. (a) (i) $\{a,b,c,d,e\}$ (ii) $\{a,b,c,g,h\}$
   (iii) $\{a,b,c,f,g,h\}$ (iv) $\{a,b,f,g,h\}$

  (b) (i) $\{c\}$ (ii) $\varnothing$
   (iii) $\{g,h\}$ (iv) $\{f\}$

  (c) (i) $\{a,b\}$ (ii) $\{d,e,f\}$
   (iii) $\{b,g,h\} = C$ (iv) $\{c,d,e,g,h\}$

  (d) (i) $\{a,b,d,e\}$ (ii) $\{a,c,g,h\}$
   (iii) $\{a,c,g,h\}$ (iv) $\{b,c,f\}$

2. (a)

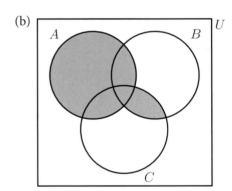

  (b)

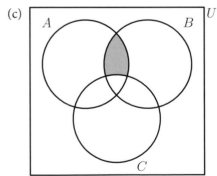

  (c)

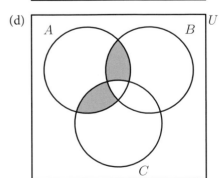

  (d)

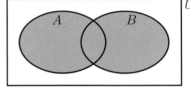

  (e)

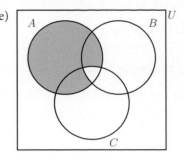

3. (a) $\mathbb{U}$ (left and right)
  (b) $\varnothing$ (left and right)
  (c) $\varnothing$ (is the left-absorbing element, there is no right-absorbing element.)
  (d) No absorbing element

8. (a)

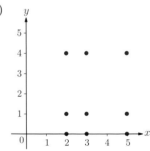

$$(A \cup B)' = A' \cap B'$$

9. (a) (i) $\mathbb{Z}^+$
    (ii) Positive even integers
    (iii) Multiples of 6
    (iv) Odd multiples of 3

Mixed examination practice 2

3. (b) $\begin{pmatrix} 1 \\ 1 \end{pmatrix}, \begin{pmatrix} \frac{1}{a} \\ \frac{1}{b} \end{pmatrix}$ (c) Associative and commutative

8. (a) 1   (b) Associative, closed, not commutative

◼ Chapter 3

Exercise 3A

1. (a) $\{(0,2),(0,3),(4,2),(4,3)\}$
  (b) $\{(1,1),(2,1),(3,1)\}$

2. (a)

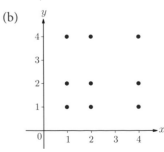

  (b)

3. (a) $\{(b,i),(b,o),(b,u),(c,i),(c,o),$
$(c,u),(d,i),(d,o),(d,u)\}$

(b) $\{(a,1),(a,4),(e,1),(e,4)\}$

(c) $\{(a,1),(a,4),(e,1),(e,4)\}$

4. (a) At least one option appears on both starter and main course lists

(b) A meal deal may be one of:
Starter + non-starter main course
Starter + dessert
Main + dessert

(c) There are no three-course meal deals.

5. False when $B = \varnothing$

Exercise 3B

1. (a) (i) Domain {0, 1, 2, 3}, Range {0, 1, 2, 4}

(ii) Domain $\{3,4,6,8\}$, Range $\{1,3,5\}$

(b) (i) Domain $\{1,3,5,7\}$, Range $\{0,1,2,3\}$

(ii) Domain $\{-1,0,1,2,3\}$, Range $\{-1,0,3\}$

(c) (i) Domain $\{1,2,3\}$, Range $\{3,4,5,6\}$

(ii) Domain $\{a,b,d,f\}$,
Range$\{big,bad,wolf\}$

2. (a) (i) $\{(1,1),(1,5),(1,9),$
$(3,3),(3,7),(3,11)\}$

(ii) $\{(1,5),(2,11),(3,7),$
$(4,3)\}$

(b) (i) $\{(1,9),(2,9),(3,3),$
$(3,9),(4,9)\}$

(ii) $\{(2,3),(2,9),(4,3),$
$(4,9)\}$

Exercise 3C

1. (a) (i) Domain $\{0,2,3\}$, Range $\{1,2,3\}$

(ii) Domain $\{1,2,3,4\}$, Range $\{-1,1,2\}$

(b) (i) Domain $\{1,2,3,4\}$, Range $\{2,3,4\}$

(ii) Domain $\{1,4,5\}$, Range $\{1,4,5\}$

(c) (i) Domain $\mathbb{R}$, Range $[-1.1]$

(ii) Domain $\mathbb{R}$, Range $[-1,\infty[$

2. (a) $\{(5, 2), (6, 2), (6, 3)\}$

(b) $\{(3,-1),(5,-1),(5,1),(7,-1),$
$(7,1),(7,3)\}$

3. (a) (i) Symmetric
(ii) Transitive

(b) (i) Symmetric
(ii) Reflexive, Transitive

(c) (i) Reflexive
(ii) Reflexive, Symmetric, Transitive

4. (a) Symmetric

(b) Reflexive, Symmetric, Transitive

(c) None

(d) Reflexive, Transitive

5. (a) Equivalence

(b) Not transitive

(c) Not transitive or reflexive

(d) Not transitive

(e) Equivalence

(f) Not symmetric

6. (b) $\{(5\cos\theta, 5\sin\theta)|\theta \in]-\pi,\pi]\}$ or
$\{(x,y)\,|\,x^2 + y^2 = 25\}$

(c) Plane partitioned into concentric circles, centred at origin.

7. (b) 2 classes:
$\hat{0} = \{3,6,9,\ldots\} = \{3n\,|\,n \in \mathbb{Z}^+\}$,
$\hat{1} = \{1,2,4,5,7,8,\ldots\} = \mathbb{Z}^+ \setminus \hat{0}$

8. (a) No

(c) $\hat{x} = \{x, 6-x\}$ for all $x \in \mathbb{R}$

(d) {3}

Exercise 3D

1. (a) (i) $[-13,\infty[$ (ii) $[-7,-1]$

(b) (i) $[-2,\infty[$ (ii) $]-\infty,\infty[$

2. (a) (i) Function
(ii) Surjection

(b) (i) Not function
(ii) Bijection

(c) (i) Bijection
(ii) Surjection

(d) (i) Not function
(ii) Function

3. (a) Injective

(b) Surjective

(c) None

(d) Bijective

4. (a) Bijection:
$$f^{-1}(x) = \sqrt[3]{\frac{1+x}{2}}$$

(b) Bijection:
$$f^{-1}(x) = \frac{(2x+1)(-1)^x - 1}{4}$$

5. (a) $f \circ g(x) = 2x - 3, g \circ f(x) = 2x - 6$

(b) $f \circ g(x) = 12 - x, g \circ f(x) = -x - 2$

(c) $f \circ g(x) = \frac{5x}{2} - 1 = g \circ f(x)$

6. Untrue, g and h may have different domains

7. (c) $f^{-1}(x,y) = \left(\frac{2y-x}{3}, \frac{x+y}{3}\right)$

8. (b) $g^{-1}(x,y) = \left(\frac{x+y}{4}, \frac{3x-y}{4}\right)$

(c) Not injective, not surjective

9. (a) range $= [-16, \infty[$, not injective

(b) $h(x) = \begin{cases} x^2 + 4x - 12 & \text{for } 0 \le x \le 2 \\ x^2 - 4x + 4 & \text{for } 2 \le x < \infty \end{cases}$

$h^{-1}(x) = \begin{cases} \sqrt{x+16} - 2 & \text{for } -12 \le x \le 0 \\ 2 + \sqrt{x} & \text{for } 0 \le x < \infty \end{cases}$

Mixed examination practice 3

1. (b)

3. (b) 6 classes:

$\hat{1} = \{1, 9, 11, 19, \ldots\} = \{5 \pm 4 + 10n \mid n \in \mathbb{N}\}$

$\hat{2} = \{2, 8, 12, 18, \ldots\} = \{5 \pm 3 + 10n \mid n \in \mathbb{N}\}$

$\hat{3} = \{3, 7, 13, 17, \ldots\} = \{5 \pm 2 + 10n \mid n \in \mathbb{N}\}$

$\hat{4} = \{4, 6, 14, 16, \ldots\} = \{5 \pm 1 + 10n \mid n \in \mathbb{N}\}$

$\hat{5} = \{5, 15, 25, \ldots\} = \{5 + 10n \mid n \in \mathbb{N}\}$

$\hat{10} = \{10, 20, 30, \ldots\} = \{10n \mid n \in \mathbb{N}\}$

4. f: surjective; not injective
g: injective; not surjective

5. (b) $\{2, 4, 8, 10, 14\}$ and $\{6, 12\}$

7. (a) Range of f is $y > 2$
(b) Show that g is injective and surjective;
$g^{-1}(u, v) = (-u + 2v, 2u - 3v)$
(c) (i) not injective; (x, y) and (y, x) have the same image
(ii) not surjective; $(0, a)$ is not in image for $a \ne 0$, e.g. $(0, 1)$

8. (c) gcd $(3, 15) = 3$
gcd $(15, 20) = 5$
but gcd $(3, 20) = 1$

9. (a) $A = [e^{-1} + 1, e + 1]$
(c) No. Range of $f \subset \mathbb{R}$
(d) $\dfrac{\pi}{2}$
(e) $g^{-1}(x) = \arcsin \ln(1 + y)$
(f) A

10. (a) $a = 0, b = 1$

Chapter 4

Exercise 4A

2. (a) Not associative
(b) Group
(c) Group
(d) Group
(e) No inverse for 0
(f) Group

3. (a)

*	0	1	2	3	4	5
0	2	3	4	5	0	1
1	3	4	5	0	1	2
2	4	5	0	1	2	3
3	5	0	1	2	3	4
4	0	1	2	3	4	5
5	1	2	3	4	5	0

(b) Group

5. $q : x \mapsto \dfrac{1}{1-x}, \ s : x \mapsto 1 - \dfrac{1}{x}, \ t : x \mapsto \dfrac{x}{x-1}$

∘	i	d	r	q	s	t
i	i	d	r	q	s	t
d	d	i	s	t	r	q
r	r	q	i	d	t	s
q	q	r	t	s	i	d
s	s	t	d	i	q	r
t	t	s	q	r	d	i

6. (a)

*	a	b	c	d
a	b	c	d	a
b	c	d	a	b
c	d	a	b	c
d	a	b	c	d

(b) d
(c) a

Exercise 4B

1. (a) 1
(b) 6
(c) 2
(d) 1
(e) ∞

2. (a) Not a group: no inverses
(b) Group, not cyclic
(c) Not a group: not closed
(d) Not a group: 0 has no inverse
(e) Cyclic group: generators 1, 5
(f) Cyclic group: generators 2, 3
(g) Group, not cyclic
(h) Not a group: 0 has no inverse
(i) Not a group: not associative

3. (a) Cyclic, 3, 7
   (b) Cyclic, 2, 8
   (c) Non-cyclic

4. (a) (i) 3   (ii) 6
   (b) 2   (c) 3

Exercise 4C

1. $\{0,1,2,3,4,5\}, \{0,2,4\}, \{0,3\}, \{0\}$

3. Line parallel to the real axis.
   e.g. $\{r+i \mid r \in \mathbb{R}\}$

4. (a) (i), (iii)
   (b) (i) $\mathbb{Q}^-$ (iii) $\left\{-\dfrac{2^m}{3} \mid m \in \mathbb{Z}\right\}$

5. $\{1, -1\}$

6. (a) $\{3, 11, 19, 27\}$
   (b) $\{5, 13, 21, 29\}$
   (c) $\{0, 8, 16, 24\}$

7. (b) $\{5, 7\}$

8. (c) G is the set of points in the plane
   $x + y - 2z = 0$

   Each coset represents a parallel plane.

13. (b) $\{1, 6\}$
   (c) $\{1, 6\}, \{2, 5\}, \{3, 4\}$

14. (b) $\left\{2, 1 + i\sqrt{3}, 1 - i\sqrt{3}\right\}$

16. (b)

$*$	e	a	b	b^2	$a*b$	$b*a$
e	e	a	b	b^2	$a*b$	$b*a$
a	a	e	$a*b$	$b*a$	b	b^2
b	b	$b*a$	b^2	e	a	$a*b$
b^2	b^2	$a*b$	e	b	$b*a$	b
$a*b$	$a*b$	b^2	$b*a$	a	e	a
$b*a$	$b*a$	b	a	$a*b$	b^2	e

   (d) $\{b*a, b\}$
   (e) $\{b^2, b*a\}$

Exercise 4D

1. $1: \{e\}$

   $2: \{e,x\}, \{e,y\}, \{e,z\}$

   $3: \{e,r,s\}$

   $6: D_3$

   No subgroups of order 4 or 5, by Lagrange's theorem

2. (a) $1, 2, 3, 6, 18$
   (b) $2, 3, 4, 6, 8, 12$

3. $1, p, q, pq$

4. $G = \{0, 2, 4, 6, 8, 10\} i$

   subgroup $\{0, 4, 8\}$

6. (a)

$\otimes_7$	1	3	5	7
1	1	3	5	7
3	3	1	7	5
5	5	7	1	3
7	7	5	3	1

Exercise 4E

1. (a) (i) 6   (ii) 2

   (b) (i) $p^{-1}q = \begin{pmatrix} a & b & c & d & e \\ a & e & c & d & b \end{pmatrix}$

   (ii) 2

2. (a) (i) $\begin{pmatrix} 1 & 2 & 3 & 4 & 5 \\ 5 & 2 & 4 & 3 & 1 \end{pmatrix}$

   (ii) $\begin{pmatrix} 1 & 2 & 3 & 4 & 5 \\ 5 & 1 & 4 & 3 & 2 \end{pmatrix}$

   (iii) $\begin{pmatrix} 1 & 2 & 3 & 4 & 5 \\ 2 & 1 & 4 & 3 & 5 \end{pmatrix} = r$

   (iv) $\begin{pmatrix} 1 & 2 & 3 & 4 & 5 \\ 3 & 2 & 1 & 5 & 4 \end{pmatrix}$

   (b) (i) 3   (ii) 3
   (iii) 2   (iv) 4
   (c) (i) 2   (ii) 6
   (iii) 2   (iv) 2

   (d) (i) $\begin{pmatrix} 1 & 2 & 3 & 4 & 5 \\ 5 & 1 & 3 & 4 & 2 \end{pmatrix}$

   (ii) $\begin{pmatrix} 1 & 2 & 3 & 4 & 5 \\ 1 & 4 & 2 & 3 & 5 \end{pmatrix}$

   (iii) $\begin{pmatrix} 1 & 2 & 3 & 4 & 5 \\ 5 & 2 & 4 & 1 & 3 \end{pmatrix} = s$

   (iv) $\begin{pmatrix} 1 & 2 & 3 & 4 & 5 \\ 5 & 2 & 4 & 3 & 1 \end{pmatrix}$

3.

$\circ$	e	r	r^2	r^3	x	n	y	p
e	e	r	r^2	r^3	x	n	y	p
r	r	r^2	r^3	e	p	x	n	y
r^2	r^2	r^3	e	r	y	p	x	n
r^3	r^3	e	r	r^2	n	y	p	x
x	x	n	y	p	e	r	r^2	r^3
n	n	y	p	x	r^3	e	r	r^2
y	y	p	x	n	r^2	r^3	e	r
p	p	x	n	y	r	r^2	r^3	e

   where x, y indicate reflection through the x-, y- axes, and p, n indicate reflection through $y = \pm x$.

4. (a) $e = \begin{pmatrix} a & b & c & d \\ a & b & c & d \end{pmatrix}$

   (b) 3

   (c) $q = \begin{pmatrix} a & b & c & d \\ b & c & a & d \end{pmatrix}$

5.
(a) $(C_1 D_1 H_1 G_1)(C_2 D_3 H_2 G_3)(C_3 D_2 H_3 G_2)$

(b) $(B_2 G_3 B_1 G_2 B_3 G_1)(D_2 C_3 D_3 C_2 D_1 C_1)$

(c) Swap and twist blocks B and G and blocks C and D.

(d) All blocks would be in their original positions, but B, G, C and D would have twisted.

Exercise 4F

1. (a) (i), (iii), (iv)

(b) (i) Unit circle $\{e^{i\theta} \mid \theta \in [0,2\pi[\}$

(iii) Positive real line $]0,\infty[$

(iv) $\{0\}$

2. (a) (i) 0 (ii) $\dfrac{2+i}{3}$ (iv) $\dfrac{2q+qi}{3}$

(b) Injective.

5. (a) (i) 9 (ii) $\{0,4\}$

(iii) $\{2,6\}$

(b) (i) $\{1,9\}$ (ii) $\{0,2,4,6\}$

6. $\ker(f) = D_3$ or $\{e,r,s\}$

$$n(\ker(f)) = \frac{n(D_3)}{n(\text{range}(f))}$$

$n(\text{range}(f)) = 1$ or 2, so the kernel must contain 3 or 6 elements of D_3

Kernel is a subgroup.

Exercise 4G

1. Function $f: G \to H$ is an isomorphism between G and H if it is bijective and $f(g_1 \star g_2) = f(g_1) \circ f(g_2)$ for all $g_1, g_2 \in G$

5. (a) 7 and 7^5 have order 6

7^2 and 7^4 have order 3

7^3 has order 2

7^6 has order 1.

(b) Isomorphism $f: A \to B$ given by $f(7^n) = 6 - n$ or $f(7^n) = n \pmod 6$.

6. (a) $p_5 = \begin{pmatrix} 1 & 2 & 3 & 4 & 5 \\ 1 & 2 & 4 & 3 & 5 \end{pmatrix}$

$p_6 = \begin{pmatrix} 1 & 2 & 3 & 4 & 5 \\ 5 & 1 & 4 & 3 & 2 \end{pmatrix}$

$\circ$	p_1	p_2	p_3	p_4	p_5	p_6
p_1	p_4	p_1	p_6	p_2	p_3	p_5
p_2	p_1	p_2	p_3	p_4	p_5	p_6
p_3	p_6	p_3	p_4	p_5	p_1	p_2
p_4	p_2	p_4	p_5	p_1	p_6	p_3
p_5	p_3	p_5	p_1	p_6	p_2	p_4
p_6	p_5	p_6	p_2	p_3	p_4	p_1

(b) Cyclic. Generators p_3 and p_6

9. (a) Not bijective

(b) Does not preserve operations. Alternatively, observe that there is no element in $\{\mathbb{R}^+, \times\}$ with order 2, but that -1 has order 2 in $\{\mathbb{R}\setminus\{0\}, \times\}$; the two groups cannot therefore be isomorphic.

10. (a)

$\circ$	D	d	r	e
D	e	r	d	D
d	r	e	D	d
r	d	D	e	r
e	D	d	r	e

(c) No. S is Klein, $\{\{1,-1,i,-i\}, \times\}$ is cyclic.

11. (b) Not isomorphisms; order not preserved

12. (b) F_5 with F_{10}, F_8 with F_{12}

Mixed examination practice 4

2. (a)

$\otimes_{20}$	1	9	11	19
1	1	9	11	19
9	9	1	19	11
11	11	19	1	9
19	19	11	9	1

$\otimes_{20}$	1	3	7	9
1	1	3	7	9
3	3	9	1	7
7	7	1	9	3
9	9	7	3	1

(c) (i) 9 (ii) 9

(d) No; all elements in G have order 2, that is not the case in H.

3. (a)

Element	1	2	3	4
Order	1	4	4	2

(b) Yes; there is an element of order 4.

6. (a) $s = \dfrac{x}{x-1}$

(c)

$\circ$	p	q	r	s
p	p	q	r	s
q	q	p	s	r
r	r	s	p	q
s	s	r	q	p

7. (c) $A_{-\theta}$

9. (c) Not Abelian

11. (a) $f(a)=2,8; f(b)=6;\ f(c)=8,2; f(d)=4$
    (b) Multiplication (modulo 10)

12. (a) 3, 6, or 12
    (b) $\{e, r^3, r^6, r^9\}$

14. (c) (i) G is a group such that there exists $a \in G$, for which
    $$G = \{a^n : n \in \mathbb{Z}\}$$
    (ii) Generators are 3 and 5
    (d) $\{1, 13\}$ and $\{1, 9, 11\}$

15. (d) (ii) $\{e, a, a^2, a^3\}$, $\{e, a^2, b * a, b * a^3\}$,
    $\{e, a^2, b, b * a^2\}$

16. (b)

$\otimes_{15}$	1	2	4	8
1	1	2	4	8
2	2	4	8	1
4	4	8	1	2
8	8	1	2	4

    (c) 1 has order 1
    2, 8 have order 4
    4 has order 2

17. (a)

$*$	A	B	C	D
A	B	A	D	C
B	A	B	C	D
C	D	C	A	B
D	C	D	B	A

    (b) e.g. $\{0, 1, 2, 3\}$ with addition modulo 4.

Chapter 5

Mixed examination practice 5

2. (b) The unit circle

3. (a)

$\otimes_{14}$	1	3	5	9	11	13
1	1	3	5	9	11	13
3	3	9	1	13	5	11
5	5	1	11	3	13	9
9	9	13	3	11	1	5
11	11	5	13	1	9	3
13	13	11	9	5	3	1

    (b) (i)

Element	1	3	5	9	11	13
Order	1	6	6	3	3	2

    (ii) 11   (iii) $\{1, 9, 11\}$

4. (a) $A, \varnothing$
    (c) No inverses

5. (b) Yes

6. (c) No; no identity

7. (a) 4
    (b) 6
    (c) 4

9. (a) $g(x) = \dfrac{1-x}{1-2x}, gg(x) = x$
    (b) $k = 1/2$
    (c) $e(x) = x, h(x) = \dfrac{2x-1}{2x}$

$\circ$	e	f	g	h
e	e	f	g	h
f	f	g	h	e
g	g	h	e	f
h	h	e	f	g

11. (a) Each row and each column contains each element exactly once.
    (b) $x = 8$
    (c) (i) 2 and 5
    (ii) $\{1, 8\}$ and $\{1, 4, 7\}$

12. (a) $\{e, y, y^2\}$
    (b) 3
    (c) $(xy)^2 = x^2 y^2$
    (d) $\{e, x, y, x^2, y^2, xy, xy^2, x^2 y, x^2 y^2\}$

13. (c) $\{p^2, pq\}$

Glossary

Words that appear in **bold** in the definitions of other terms are also defined in this glossary. The abstract nature of this option means that some defined terms can realistically only be explained in terms of other, more simple concepts.

Term	Definition	Example
Abelian group	A **group** whose **binary operation** is **commutative** over the elements of the group.	Any cyclic group is Abelian.
absolute complement	All elements of the **universal set** not present in the given set.	In $\mathbb{Z}$, the absolute complement of the set of even numbers is the set of odd numbers.
associative	A **binary operation** $*$ is associative if multiple instances of the operation can be resolved in any order without affecting the outcome: $x*(y*z)=(x*y)*z$ for all x, y and z	Addition is associative over $\mathbb{R}$: $(x+y)+z=x+(y+z)$ for all $x, y, z \in \mathbb{R}$.
bijection	A function which is both *injective* and *surjective*.	The function $f: \mathbb{R} \to \mathbb{R}$ given by $f: x \mapsto x+1$ is a bijection.
binary operation	An operation $*$ which takes two elements (arguments) and produces a single element.	Addition in $\mathbb{R}$ is a binary operation.
cancellation	For an **associative binary operation** $*$, if the inverse x^{-1} of an element x exists, then equation $y*x=z*x$ can be simplified to $y=z$ by right-cancellation, and $x*a=x*b$ can be simplified to $a=b$ by left-cancellation. For a **commutative** operation, the left- and right- specification is redundant.	Because the multiplicative inverse of 4 exists in $\mathbb{R}$, we can simplify $4x = 24$ to $x = 6$.
cardinality	The number of elements in a set. Also called **size**.	The cardinality of $\{1, 2, 3, 7, 9\}$ is 5.
Cartesian product	The Cartesian product of two sets A and B is denoted $A \times B$ and consists of all possible **ordered pairs** (a,b) where $a \in A$ and $b \in B$.	The Cartesian product of $\{1, 2\}$ and $\{3, 4, 7\}$ is $\{(1,3),(1,4),(1,7),(2,3),(2,4),(2,7)\}$.
Cayley table	The grid array with set elements listed in the title row and column cells, where each internal cell is the result of performing a given set operation on the title elements.	The Cayley table for $\wedge$ on set $\{1, 2, 3, 4\}$ is: | $\wedge$	1	2	3	4
---	---	---	---	---
1	1	1	1	1
2	2	4	8	16
3	3	9	27	81
4	4	16	64	256	
closed	A set S is closed under a **binary operation** $*$ if for any elements x and y in S, their resultant $x*y$ is also in S.	$\mathbb{Z}$ is closed under addition.

Term	Definition	Example
codomain	For a **relation** or function $f: A \rightarrow B$, the codomain is B.	For function $f: \mathbb{Z} \rightarrow \mathbb{Z}$ given by $f(x) = |x| + 1$, the codomain is $\mathbb{Z}$, but the range is $\mathbb{Z}^+$.
commutative	A **binary operation** $*$ is commutative over set S if for all $x, y \in S$: $x * y = y * x$	Addition is commutative in $\mathbb{R}$, but subtraction is not.
complement	Shorthand for **absolute complement**. See also **set difference**.	In $\mathbb{Z}$, the complement of the set of even numbers is the set of odd numbers.
composition	Application of a function to the output of another function. Composition is **associative**.	The composition of $f: x \mapsto x^2$ with $g: x \mapsto x + 3$ is $f \circ g: x \mapsto (x+3)^2$.
congruence modulo n	For integers x and y and positive integer n, x and y are congruent modulo n if $(x - y)$ is an integer multiple of n.	7 and 19 are congruent modulo 4 because $(7 - 19) = 4 \times (-3)$.
cosets	For a **group** $\{H, *\}$ with **subgroup** G and element $a \in H$, $h * G$ is a **subset** of H given as $a * G = \{a * g \mid g \in G\}$ and is called the left coset of G, determined by a. Similarly, $G * a$ is called the right coset of G, determined by a.	For subgroup $G = \{1, i, -1, -i\}$ of $\{\mathbb{C} \setminus \{0\}, \times\}$, the left coset $(1 - i) \times G = \{(1-i), (1+i), (-1+i), (-1-i)\}$.
cyclic group	A cyclic **group** has a *generating* element a such that each element of the group can be expressed as a^n for some integer value of n.	The group of rotational symmetries of any regular polygon is a cyclic group.
De Morgan's laws	Paired facts relating to set operations: • The **union** of *complements* is the **complement** of the **intersection**. $A' \cup B' = (A \cap B)'$ • The **intersection** of *complements* is the **complement** of the **union**. $A' \cap B' = (A \cup B)'$	
dihedral group of order n	The **group** of *symmetries* of a regular n-gon, usually denoted D_n.	D_3 is the six-element group for the symmetries of an equilateral triangle: Rotations by $0°$, $120°$ and $-120°$, and reflections through each of the symmetry lines connecting a vertex to the midpoint of the opposite side.
direct proof	Proof which uses known facts to construct the desired result.	Direct proof for the formula of the sum of a finite geometric series: Let $$S_n = \sum_{i=0}^{n-1} ar^i$$ Then $$(r-1)S_n = \sum_{i=0}^{n-1} ar^{i+1} - \sum_{i=0}^{n-1} ar^i$$ $$= \sum_{i=1}^{n} ar^i - \sum_{i=0}^{n-1} ar^i$$ $$= ar^n - a$$ Hence, for $r \neq 1$, $$S_n = \frac{a(r^n - 1)}{r - 1}$$
disjoint	Two sets which share no common element are disjoint.	$\{1, 2, 3\}$ and $\{4, 5, 6\}$ are disjoint.

Term	Definition	Example
distributive	For two **binary operations** $*$ and $\circ$ on a set S, $*$ is distribute over $\circ$ if $x*(y \circ z) = (x*y) \circ (x*z)$ for all $y, z \in S$.	Multiplication is distributive over addition in $\mathbb{R}$: $x(y+z) = xy + xz$.
domain	For a **relation** $f : A \rightarrow B$, the domain is A. If f is a function, it can be assumed that f is defined over all elements of A. Where not explicitly stated, the domain of a numerical function is taken to be the maximal **subset** of $\mathbb{R}$ in which the function is defined.	The function $f : x \mapsto \dfrac{1}{x-1}$ has domain $\mathbb{R} \setminus \{1\}$.
equivalence class	For an **equivalence relation** R, the equivalence class $\hat{x}$ is the set of all elements equivalent to x: $x = \{y \mid xRy\}$.	$\{6n + 1\}$ is an equivalence class under the relation congruence modulo 6.
equivalence relation	An equivalence relation is a **binary operation** which is **reflexive**, **symmetric** and **transitive**.	Congruence modulo n is an equivalence class in $\mathbb{Z}$ for any positive integer n.
finite group	A **group** with a finite number of elements.	The group of symmetries of a square is a finite group with six elements.
generator	An element a of a group with the property that every element of the group can be expressed as a^n for some integer value of n.	i is a generator of the group $\{1, i, -1, -i\}$ under multiplication.
group	Group $\{G, *\}$ consists of a set G under a **binary operator** $*$, which fulfils the four group axioms • **associativity** • **closure** • **identity** • **inverses**	$\{1, -1\}$ forms a group under multiplication. $\{1, 0, -1\}$ does not form a group under multiplication, since element 0 has no inverse in the set.
homomorphism	A function mapping elements of one **group** to another group which preserves group operations.	$f : x \mapsto 2x$ is a homomorphism from $\{\mathbb{Z}_8, \oplus_8\}$ to $\{\mathbb{Z}_{16}, \oplus_{16}\}$.
identity element	The unique element e for a given **binary operation** $*$, such that $x*e = e*x = x$ for any x.	In $\mathbb{R}$, the multiplicative identity is 1 and the additive identity is 0.
indirect proof	A means of supplying a desired result by rigorous argument which demonstrates its necessary validity.	Examples include proof by induction and proof by contradiction.
infinite group	A **group** with infinitely many elements.	$\{\mathbb{Z}, +\}$ is an infinite group.
injection	A function $f : A \rightarrow B$ where each element of A maps to a distinct element of B: $f(x) = f(y)$ only if $x = y$.	$f : \mathbb{R} \rightarrow \mathbb{R}$ given by $f : x \mapsto x+1$ is an injection; $g : \mathbb{R} \rightarrow \mathbb{R}$ given by $g : x \mapsto x^2$ is not an injection, since $g(-1) = g(1)$.
intersection	The set of elements common to two given sets. Intersection is denoted by the symbol $\cap$.	The intersection of $\{1, 2, 3\}$ and $\{1, 3, 5\}$ is $\{1, 3\}$.
inverse function	For a **bijection** $f : A \rightarrow B$, the inverse function f^{-1} has the property that $f(x) = y \Leftrightarrow f^{-1}(y) = x$.	For $f : x \mapsto 2x + 1$, the inverse function is $f^{-1} : x \mapsto \dfrac{x-1}{2}$.

Term	Definition	Example
isomorphism	A *bijective* **homomorphism.**	Function $f : x \mapsto \ln x$ is an isomorphism from $\{\mathbb{R} \setminus \{0\}, \times\}$ to $\{\mathbb{R}, +\}$.
kernel	For a **homomorphism** $f : G \to H$, the kernel is the set of elements in G which are mapped by f to the *identity* of H. $\ker(f) = \{g \in G \mid f(g) = e_H\}$ The kernel is always a **subgroup** of the *domain group*.	Isomorphism $f : \{\mathbb{Z}_{12}, \oplus_{12}\} \to \{\mathbb{Z}_4, \oplus_4\}$ is given by $f(x) = x$ (*modulo* 4). Then $\ker(f) = \{0, 4, 8\}$.
Klein four-group	The **group** structure of a four-element group, each element of which is self-inverse.	The set $\{1, 3, 5, 7\}$ under multiplication modulo 8 forms a Klein four-group.
Lagrange's theorem	For any **subgroup** G of a **finite group** H, $n(G)$ is a divisor of $n(H)$.	
Latin square	A table has the Latin square property if each element appears exactly once in each row and once in each column. The Latin square property is a necessary but not sufficient condition for a **Cayley table** to represent a **group**.	The Cayley table below has the Latin square property, but could not represent a group, since no element could be the identity. 	$*$	a	b	c	d	 |---|---|---|---|---| 	a	c	b	a	d	 	b	b	a	d	c	 	c	a	d	c	b	 	d	d	c	b	a	
order	The *order of a group* is the number of elements in that group. The *order of an element* a is the least positive integer n such that $a^n = e$, the identity element.	The order of group $\{\mathbb{Z}_9, \oplus_9\}$ is 9. The order of element 6 under addition modulo 9 is 3, since $6 \oplus_9 6 \oplus_9 6 = 0$, the additive identity.
ordered pairs	An ordered pair is any element of a **Cartesian product** $A \times B$, consisting of an element from one set A and one element from set B, given in that order with a comma separation and enclosed in rounded brackets.	$(2, 4)$, $(5, 5)$ and $(7, -1)$ are all ordered pairs drawn from $\mathbb{Z}^2$.
partition	A partition of a set is any fragmentation of that set into *disjoint subsets*. Sets $A_1, A_2, \ldots$ are said to partition set B if: • $A_i \cap A_j = \varnothing$ for all $i \neq j$ • $A_1 \cup A_2 \cup \ldots = B$	The odd integers and the even integers partition $\mathbb{Z}$.
power	The number of elements in a set. Also called **size**.	The power of $\{1, 2, 3, 7, 9\}$ is 5.
proof by contradiction	A method of proof which works by assuming the desired result is untrue and demonstrating that this leads to an impossibility or an internal contradiction.	The proof that $\sqrt{2}$ is irrational is given as an example in chapter 1.

Term	Definition	Example
proof by induction	A method of proving that a result is true for all positive integer values of a particular parameter. By explicitly demonstrating the validity of one or more 'base cases' and then demonstrating that each case can be shown to prove the validity of the subsequent case, the result is considered proved for all cases.	Proof that $$\sum_{r=1}^{n} r^2 = \frac{n(n+1)(2n+1)}{6}$$ Base case: $n=1$: $$\sum_{r=1}^{1} r^2 = 1^2 = \frac{1(1+1)(2+1)}{6}$$ So the result is true for $n=1$. Inductive step: Assume true for $n=k$, so $$\sum_{r=1}^{k} r^2 = \frac{k(k+1)(2k+1)}{6}$$ Then when $n=k+1$: $$\sum_{r=1}^{k+1} r^2 = \sum_{r=1}^{k} r^2 + (k+1)^2$$ $$= \frac{k(k+1)(2k+1)}{6} + (k+1)^2$$ $$= \frac{k+1}{6}\left(2k^2 + k + 6(k+1)\right)$$ $$= \frac{k+1}{6}\left(2k^2 + 7k + 6\right)$$ $$= \frac{(k+1)(k+2)(2k+3)}{6}$$ $$= \frac{(k+1)\left((k+1)+1\right)\left(2(k+1)+1\right)}{6}$$ The result is true for $n=k+1$. So the result is true for $n=1$ and if true for $n=k$, it is also true for $n=k+1$. Therefore this result is true for all $n \in \mathbb{Z}^+$ by the principle of mathematical induction.
proper	A proper **subset** is any subset other than the **trivial** subsets (the original set and the empty set). A proper **subgroup** is any subgroup other than the **trivial** subgroups (the original group and the group consisting only of the identity element).	$\{1, 3\}$ is a proper subset of $\{0, 1, 2, 3, 4, 5\}$. $\{\{1,-1\}, \times\}$ is a proper subgroup of $\{\mathbb{R} \setminus \{0\}, \times\}$.
range	The range of a **relation** or function $f: A \rightarrow B$ is the set of all elements of B appearing as right-components of elements of the relation: range $= \{b \mid (a,b) \in f \text{ for some } a \in A\}$ If f is a function, the range is more simply defined as the set of values $\{f(a) \mid a \in A\}$.	Functions $f, g : \mathbb{R}^+ \rightarrow \mathbb{R}$ are given by $f : x \mapsto x^2$ $g : x \mapsto \ln x$ The range of f is $\mathbb{R}^+$. The range of g is $\mathbb{R}$.
reflexive	A **relation** R is reflexive in a set S if, for all x in S: xRx	$\leq$ is a reflexive relation in $\mathbb{R}$.
relation	A (binary) relation is a set of **ordered pairs**, usually generated according to an underlying rule.	For set $S = \{1, 2, 3, 4, 5\}$, the relation $R \subset S \times S$ is defined by $aRb \Leftrightarrow a^2 > 7b$ Then $R = \{(3,1), (4,1), (4,2), (5,1), (5,2), (5,3)\}$.

Term	Definition	Example
self-inverse	An element a is self-inverse under a **binary operation** $*$ if $a*a=e$, the **identity element**.	Under composition of functions, $f:x \mapsto 1-x$ is self-inverse.
set difference	Those elements of one set which are not present in a second set. Set difference is given with a $\backslash$ symbol.	$\{1,2,3,4\} \backslash \{1,4,5,6\} = \{2,3\}$.
size	The number of elements in a set.	The size of set $\{1, 2, 3, 7, 9\}$ is 5.
subgroup	A **subset** of the elements of a **group** which itself satisfies the conditions to be a group under the same operator.	$\{\{1,-1\},\times\}$ is a subgroup of $\{\mathbb{R} \backslash \{0\},\times\}$.
subset	A set of elements drawn from a given set.	$\{1,2\}$ is a subset of $\{1,2,3,6\}$. $\{1,4\}$ is not a subset of $\{1,2,3,6\}$.
superset	A set of elements containing all the elements of a given set.	$\{1,2,3,6\}$ is a superset of $\{1,2\}$. $\{1,2,3,6\}$ is not a superset of $\{1,2\}$.
surjection	A function whose **range** is the whole of its **codomain**. $f:A \to B$ and for every $b \in B$, there is at least one element $a \in A$ such that $f(a)=b$.	Functions $f,g:\mathbb{Z} \to \mathbb{Z}$ are given by $f(x)=x+3$ and $g(x)=2x$. $f(x)$ is a surjection, $g(x)$ is not a surjection.
symmetric	A **relation** R is symmetric in a set S if, for any x and y in S: xRy whenever yRx	Similarity is a symmetric relation in the set of all triangles.
symmetric difference	The set of elements present in only one of two given sets. Symmetric difference is given with the Δ symbol.	$\{1,2,3,4\} \Delta \{1,4,5,6\} = \{2,3,5,6\}$.
symmetry	Any transformation of a shape which maps it so that each edge coincides with one of the initial edge positions.	A non-square rectangle has two reflective symmetries and two rotational symmetries.
transitive	A **relation** R is transitive in a set S if, for any x, y and z in S: if xRy and yRz, then xRz.	'is a factor of' is a transitive relation in $\mathbb{Z}^+$.
transposition	A permutation consisting of the exchange of two elements.	Permutation $p = \begin{pmatrix} 1 & 2 & 3 & 4 & 5 \\ 4 & 2 & 5 & 1 & 3 \end{pmatrix}$ can be written as a composition of two transpositions: $p = (14)(35)$
trivial	The trivial **subsets** of set A are A and $\varnothing$. The trivial **subgroups** of group $\{G,*\}$ are $\{G,*\}$ and $\{\{e\},*\}$.	$\{1, 3\}$ is a non-trival subset of $\{0,1,2,3,4,5\}$. $\{\{1,-1\},\times\}$ is a non-trival subgroup of $\{\mathbb{R} \backslash \{0\},\times\}$.
union	The set of elements appearing in either or both of two given sets. Union is denoted by the symbol $\cup$.	The union of $\{1,2,3\}$ and $\{1,3,5,7\}$ is $\{1,2,3,5,7\}$.

Term	Definition	Example
universal set	The set of all elements under consideration, denoted U. If not explicitly defined, U will usually be clear from context as either $\mathbb{Z}$ or $\mathbb{R}$. The universal set must be known if an **absolute complement** is to be determined.	If $U = \{1, 2, 3, 4, 5, 6\}$ and $A = \{1, 5\}$ then $A' = \{2, 3, 4, 6\}$.

Index

Abelian group, 68
    definition, 134
absolute complement, 9, 33
    definition, 134
additive identity, 17
associativity
    binary operations, 19–21
    composition of functions, 58
    definition, 134
    group axiom, 68, 72–73, 93
    property of intersection, 26
    property of union, 25
    symmetric difference, 28

bijectivity
    definition, 134
    functions, 55, 56, 63
    isomorphisms, 110, 115
binary operations, 12–22
    definition, 134
    on sets, 25–32
binary relations, 40–42

cancellation, definition, 134
cancellation laws, groups, 71–74
cardinality of a set, 7
    definition, 134
Cartesian product, 38, 40, 62
    definition, 134
Cayley tables, 13–14, 67, 69
    cyclic groups, 76
    definition, 134
    Klein four-group, 90–91
    'Latin square' property, 72–74
closure
    definition, 134
    group axiom, 68, 93
    operations, 12–14
codomain
    of a function, 52–53, 63
    of a relation, 41
    definition, 135
commutativity
    of an Abelian group, 68
    binary operations, 15, 33
    definition, 135
    inheritance of, subgroups, 81
    property of intersection, 26
    property of union, 25
    symmetric difference, 28
complementary sets, 9, 33
    intersection of, 26
    union of, 25
complement, definition, 135
composition
    of permutations, 95–96
    of transformations, 92–93
    of two functions, 57–60, 63
congruence (modulo n), 42, 62
    definition, 135

contradiction, proof by, 3–5
cosets, 81–82
    definition, 135
    properties of, 83–84
cyclic groups, 76–78
    definition, 135
    isomorphism property of, 111–12

decomposition of permutations, 97–100
De Morgan's laws, 29–31
    definition, 135
dihedral group of order n, 93, 114
    definition, 135
    groups of order 6 (D_3), 91, 126
direct proofs, 3
    definition and example, 135
disjoint
    cosets, 83
    definition, 135
    sets, 26
distributivity, 21–22
    definition, 136
    intersection and union of sets, 26
domain
    of a function, 51–53
    of a relation, 41, 42, 62
    definition, 136

empty relation, 46
empty set, 9, 10
    intersection of, 26
equivalence classes, 47–48, 63
    definition, 136
equivalence relations, 46–47, 62–63
    definition, 136

finite group, 74, 75
    definition, 136
    Lagrange's theorem, 86–87
functions, 50–51, 63
    between groups, 101–6
    classifying, 53–57
    composition of, 57–60, 63
    domain, codomain and range, 51–53
    exercises, 61–62
    mixed exam practice, 64–66
    summary, 63

Galois Theory, 95
generator element, cyclic groups, 76–78, 114
    definition, 136
geometrical transformations, groups, 91–93
groups, 67
    Abelian, 68
    cancellation laws, 71–74
    cyclic, 76–78, 111–12
    definition, 136
    four axioms of, 67–68, 93
    geometrical transformations, 91–93
    homomorphisms, 101–6

isomorphisms, 109–11
kernels, 106–8
mixed exam practice, 116–18
order of, 74–75
of order 6, 91, 125–26
permutations, 94–100
structures, 67–70, 89–91
subgroups, 79–88
summary, 114–15

homomorphisms, 101–6, 115
    definition, 136
    exercises, 108–9

identity axiom, groups, 68, 69, 93
identity element, 16–17, 33
    cyclic groups, 76
    definition, 136
    kernel of a homomorphism, 107
    subgroups, 80
identity functions, 59, 63
identity permutation, 96
image of a binary relation, 41
indirect proof, 3
    definition, 136
injectivity of functions, 53–54, 55–56, 63
    definition, 136
intersection of sets, 25–27, 33
    definition, 136
    De Morgan's laws, 29
introductory problem, 1–2, 119–20
inverse elements, 17–19, 33
inverse functions, 56–57, 59–60, 63
    definition, 136
inverse permutation, 96
inverses axiom, groups, 68, 81, 93
isomorphisms, 109–11, 115
    definition, 137
    exercises, 112–14

kernels, homomorphism, 106–8, 115
    definition, 137
Klein 4-group, 91, 93, 114
    definition, 137

Lagrange's theorem, 86–88, 114
    definition, 137
Latin square, 72–73, 76
    definition, 137

multiplicative identity, 18

number sets, 7–8
numerical congruence, 42

operations, 12
    associativity, 19–21
    closure, 12–14
    commutativity, 15
    distributivity, 21–22
    exercises, 23–25
    identity element, 16–17
    mixed exam practice, 35–36
    on sets, 25–32
    summary, 33–34

operations on groups, 101–3
    preservation of, 104–6, 112
operations on sets, 25
    De Morgan's laws, 29–31
    exercises, 31–32
    intersection, 25–27
    set difference, 27–28
    symmetric difference, 28–29
    union, 25
order of a group, 74–75
    definition, 137
    groups of orders 1 to 7, 89–91
order of a permutation, 97–98
ordered pairs, 37–40, 62
    definition, 137
order of an element, 74–75
    definition, 137
order relation, 47

partition of a set, 26, 34
    definition, 137
    by equivalence classes, 47–48
permutations, 94–95, 114–15
    composition of, 95–96
    decomposition of, 97–100
    exercises, 100–1
    identity and inverse, 96
power of a set, 7, 137
prime order groups, 78, 114
proof by contradiction, 3–5
    definition, 137
proof by induction, 3
    definition and example, 138
proper
    definition, 138
    subgroups, 80–81
    subsets, 9

range
    of a function, 52–53
    of a relation, 41, 62
    definition, 138
reflective symmetry, 91–92
reflexive relations, 43–44, 62
relations, 40–41, 43, 62–63
    definition, 138
    domain and range, 41–42
    empty, 46
    equivalence, 46–48
    exercises, 48–50
    mixed exam practice, 64–66
    reflexive, 43–44
    symmetric, 44–45
    transitive, 45–46
relative complement, 27, 28
rotational symmetry, 91–92
Russell's paradox, 8

scalar triple product, 22
self-inverse, 19, 33
    definition, 139
    permutations, 97–98
set difference, 27–28
    definition, 139

sets
    complementary, 9
    enumerating, 7
    exercises, 10–11
    mixed exam practice, 35–36
    notation for, 6–7
    operations on, 25–32
    standard number, 7–9
    subsets, 9–10
    summary, 33–34
size of a set, 7, 139
standard number sets, 7–8
subgroups, 79–81, 114
    cosets of, 81–84
    definition, 139
    exercises, 84–86
    Lagrange's theorem, 86–88
subsets, 9–10
    definition, 139
supersets, 9–10
    definition, 139
surjectivity of functions, 54, 63
    definition, 139
symmetric difference, sets, 28–29
    definition, 139
symmetric relations, 44–45, 62
    definition, 139
symmetry
    definition, 139
    geometric transformations, 91–93

transformations, geometric, 91–93
transitive relations, 45–46, 62
    definition, 139
transposition of elements, 97
    definition, 139
trivial subgroups, 80
    definition, 139

union of sets, 25, 33
    definition, 139
    De Morgan's laws, 29
    distributivity, 26
universal set, 8
    absolute complement of, 9
    definition, 140

Acknowledgements

The authors and publishers are grateful for the permissions granted to reproduce materials in either the original or adapted form. While every effort has been made, it has not always been possible to identify the sources of all the materials used, or to trace all copyright holders. If any omissions are brought to our notice, we will be happy to include the appropriate acknowledgements on reprinting.

IB exam questions © International Baccalaureate Organization. We gratefully acknowledge permission to reproduce International Baccalaureate Organization intellectual property.

Cover image: Thinkstock

Diagrams in the book were created by Ben Woolley.